the Real
CHRIST

R. A. TORREY

WHITAKER
HOUSE

Publisher's note: This book originated as a series of sermons by R. A. Torrey.

Unless otherwise indicated, all Scripture quotations are taken from the King James Version of the Holy Bible. Scripture quotations marked (RV) are taken from the Revised Version of the Holy Bible. Scripture quotation marked (ASV) is taken from the American Standard Edition of the Revised Version of the Holy Bible

THE REAL CHRIST

ISBN: 978-1-60374-725-7
eBook ISBN: 978-1-60374-726-4
Printed in the United States of America
© 2013 by Whitaker House

Whitaker House
1030 Hunt Valley Circle
New Kensington, PA 15068
www.whitakerhouse.com

Catalog-in-Publication Data (Pending)

1 2 3 4 5 6 7 8 9 10 11 **ω** 20 19 18 17 16 15 14 13

"We would see Jesus."
—John 12:21

"Then were the disciples glad, when they saw the Lord."
—John 20:20

CONTENTS

PREFACE

For years, it has been on my heart to write a book on the real Christ, the Christ of actual historic fact, as distinguished from the Christ of man's dreams and fancies and imaginings. I have spent many hours in the famous picture galleries of Europe studying the paintings of The Christ by the so-called masters and I have always been disappointed and oftentimes indignant at the gross misrepresentations of the face of Jesus Christ as they presented it. One night, I was in a world-famous center of culture and art in the Old World when a man called to see me. When he entered the room, I glanced at his face and felt certain that he was the model of many of the so-called portraits of our Lord. One of the first things he said to me confirmed my suspicion. And why had he come to see me? Because he was the slave of sin in one of its most disgusting forms and had come to find if there were any ways to be delivered from it. Yet the face of this moral degenerate was used as a model by those who would portray the countenance of the perfect Man!

The representations of Christ by many poets, essayists, and preachers, while not so grossly false, are nevertheless unsatisfying. They do not present the real Christ any more than Edwin Arnold's *Light of Asia* presented the real Buddha. Although humans may fail to artistically portray Christ, we thankfully already have a perfect portrayal of the real Christ—the Christ of God's own appointment and the Christ of actual fact, in all His many-sided and complete perfection, beauty, and glory. This portrait is found God's own Word. It is found in the preview of the coming Christ granted to the Old Testament prophets, in the histories of Christ as written by the four evangelists, and in the explanation of that picture by the inspired apostles. I have pored over that marvelous picture for many days and weeks and months and years, and my wonder continues to grow.

At a Bible conference a number of years ago, I attempted to give a series of addresses on the real Christ. A few attendees testified of the blessings they received, but I was still not satisfied. So, I studied on and prayed that I might see Him and tell of Him as He actually was. At last, I decided to attempt, by the Holy Spirit's enabling, to interpret God's own picture of Christ—the Christ of God's own appointment—to my own people and then to share this interpretation with many others through the written word. My wife is directly responsible for this decision. She delights in ministry that is instructive rather than merely hortatory, and she prefers ministry that is coherent, orderly, progressive, systematic, symmetrical, and complete in its teaching. So, she said to me one day last October as we were crossing the Pacific from China to America, "About what are you going to preach a series of sermons next winter?"

"I do not know," I replied.

"Well, you are going to preach a series of some kind, are you not?"

"I suppose so."

"Well, about what?" She was insistent, and there was no escape.

"Perhaps about the real Christ."

"I think that would be a good subject."

So I prayed, and a higher Authority said to me, "Preach on the real Christ." Then I did. I have never enjoyed preaching as much on any other topic as I have on this one. Sometimes, as I beheld His wondrous beauty while I spoke, I could hardly go on with my dictation. It happened multiple times that as I spoke, a strange, glad awe has befallen me and my hearers alike. The crowds have only since grown, and many people have been blessed and changed. May God bless the reading of these studies as He has the preaching and the hearing of them.

—R. A. Torrey

*"Let all the house of Israel know assuredly,
that God hath made that same Jesus,
whom ye have crucified, both Lord and Christ."*
—Acts 2:36

1

THE REAL CHRIST

"And the Word was made flesh, and dwelt among us, (and we beheld his glory, the glory as of the only begotten of the Father,) full of grace and truth."
—John 1:14

"But we all, with open face beholding as in a glass the glory of the Lord, are changed into the same image from glory to glory, even as by the Spirit of the Lord."
—2 Corinthians 3:18

"He that saith he abideth in him ought himself also so to walk, even as he walked."
—1 John 2:6

My subject is the real Christ, and we will be looking at the three above texts.

We hear a great deal about Christ in our day. It is doubtful there ever was an age before this in which men talked and wrote so much about Christ as they do today. We hear about "Christ" not only from thoroughly orthodox, evangelical Christians but also from Roman Catholics. We hear about "Christ" from Unitarians. We hear about "Christ" from Theosophists. We hear about "Christ" from Christian Scientists. We hear about "Christ" from Spiritualists. We hear about "Christ" from some Buddhists. We hear about "Christ" from Behaists, and we hear about "Christ" from Socialists and Anarchists. We hear about "Christ" even from men and women who make no profession whatsoever of any religion. We see His name, His title, and His sign everywhere.

But the Christ many people are talking about and urging upon men is not the real Christ. He is not the actual Christ Jesus who once walked this earth and whom men saw and studied and knew. He is not the Christ who was the incarnate Word of God and whose glory men actually saw with their own eyes, *"the glory as of the only begotten of the Father, full of grace and truth"* (John 1:14). He is not the Christ who once lived and died and was raised again. The Christ many talk about is a pure figment of their imaginations, which they have substituted for the actual Christ of history, the Christ who once lived here on earth but who now lives in glory. They have substituted a figment of their imaginations for the One who will come back some day to take the reins of government and save this wrecked and ruined human society of ours, making it what it ought to be.

The "Christ" of Christian Scientists, for example, is not the real Christ. You sometimes think, when you hear Christian Scientists talk about Christ (if you are not fully informed), that they are talking about our Lord Jesus Christ. They say that they believe in the divinity of Christ. Not for one moment do they mean that. When they talk about "Christ," they do not mean a definite person at all, any more than when they speak about "God" as being a definite person. What they really mean is the "Christ principle."

The "Christ" of Theosophy is not the real Christ. Even the "Christ" of Roman Catholicism is not the real Christ, though in some measure He is. The Roman Catholics, when they speak about Christ, are talking about the Jesus who was crucified, is risen, and is coming again. They mean a divine Jesus, but the picture they draw of Him and His character and His relation to His virgin mother is very different from the picture God has drawn in His Book. The Christ pictured in many Protestant pulpits is also not the real Christ.

The only place to see the real Christ, just as He was and is, is in His Book. Many people today say that they believe in Christ but not in the Christ of the Bible. Yet there is no other Christ than the Christ of the Bible! Any Christ other than the Christ of the Bible is a pure figment of the individual imagination, a mere idol substituted for a divine reality. It is just as much of an idol as those that men fashion with their hands out of iron, silver, gold, wood, or stone. The only difference is that it is manufactured in the mind.

The real Christ is set forth in our first text, John 1:14: "*And the Word was made flesh, and dwelt among us, (and we beheld his glory, the glory as of the only begotten of the Father,) full of grace and truth,*" and in Acts 2:36: "*Let all the house of Israel know assuredly, that God hath made that same Jesus, whom ye have crucified, both Lord and Christ.*" This man Jesus, who walked this earth more than nineteen hundred years ago and was God manifest in the flesh, is alone the real Christ. God's Book—not merely the four Gospels but the entire sixty-six books of the Bible—tells about Him. Now we will take the time to study how the real Christ is pictured in this Book.

I have said that the Bible is the only book that can help us to really and truly know Him, the real Christ. Let me add that the Holy Spirit is the only Person who can enable us to understand

Him as He is set forth in the Bible. God has drawn the picture of the real Christ in the Bible, and the Holy Spirit is God's interpreter of that holy picture. It is the work of the Holy Spirit to bear witness of the real Christ (see John 15:26 RV), and it is only as He testifies of Christ, only as He takes the picture given to us in the written Word of God and interprets it, that we come to know or understand the real Christ—Jesus Christ.

Our study of Christ is threefold:

First, that we may see Him in all His moral glory, *"the glory as of the only begotten of the Father, full of grace and truth,"* and, in response, admire and love and glorify Him as we ought.

Second, that we may become like Him by seeing who He truly is. *"But we all, with unveiled face reflecting as a mirror the glory of the Lord, are transformed into the same image from glory to glory, even as from the Lord the Spirit"* (2 Corinthians 3:18 RV).

Third, that we may have a standard for how to conduct ourselves in Christ. Or, as John puts it in our third text, *"He that saith he abideth in him ought himself also so to walk, even as he walked"* (1 John 2:6). The Ten Commandments are not the Christian's rules for life. The Christian has a far higher calling than obeying the Ten Commandments. Jesus Christ Himself is the standard we are to follow. *"He that saith he abideth in him ought himself also so to walk, even as he walked."*

Jesus Christ, the Holy One

We will look today at the most fundamental aspect of Christ's character. What do you think is the most fundamental aspect of Christ's character? Holiness! Christ is the Holy One. Holiness is the first and most preeminent characteristic of Jesus Christ that appears in the Word of God. John said in our first text, *"We beheld his glory, the glory as of the only begotten of the Father."* Now, holiness is the preeminent moral characteristic of God; therefore, it is also the preeminent characteristic of Jesus Christ. It is true what John says in 1 John 4:8: *"God is love."* But John had said something before this that provided a deep foundation for it. It is found in 1 John 1:5: *"This then is the message which we have heard of him, and declare unto you, that God is light, and in him is no darkness at all."* One of the major themes found in Old Testament revelation, which helped form the basis for New Testament revelation, was to teach, elucidate, and burn the fundamental truth of God into Jewish consciousness, namely, that God is holy. Holiness, I repeat, was and is the fundamental, preeminent moral attribute of God and today is the fundamental, preeminent moral attribute of the real Christ. Was Christ loving? Yes. Was Christ gentle and merciful? Yes. Was Christ meek and humble and prayerful? Yes. We shall study all these attributes of Christ in their place, but Christ was, first of all, holy. He was *"light, and in him is no darkness at all."*

We will divide what we have to say on the holiness of Christ into the two following sections.

The Fact of the Holiness of the Real Christ

First we will look at the fact of the holiness of the real Christ. The fact that Jesus Christ was, first of all and above all else, holy, is shown in many passages in the Bible.

The Word Depicts Jesus as Holy

First of all, in the Word, Christ's holiness is clearly, directly, and definitely asserted again and again. In Acts, we read,

For of a truth against thy holy child Jesus, whom thou hast anointed, both Herod, and Pontius Pilate, with the Gentiles, and the people of Israel, were gathered together...by stretching forth thine hand to heal; and that signs and wonders may be done by the name of thy holy child Jesus.   (Acts 4:27, 30)

The holiness of Jesus is mentioned twice here as the one complete, descriptive moral attribute of Christ Jesus.

In Mark 1:24, we read of a demon-possessed man who cried out, *"Let us alone; what have we to do with thee, thou Jesus of Nazareth? art thou come to destroy us? I know thee who thou art, the Holy One of God."* Here, a demon—a being of superior intelligence but inferior character—is compelled to declare the truth about Jesus, that He was not only holy but also *"the Holy One of God."* In Acts 3:14, we read, *"But ye denied the Holy One and the Just, and desired a murderer to be granted unto you."* Here, the apostle Peter, filled with the Holy Ghost, declares that Jesus is *"the Holy One."* In 1 John 2:20, we read, *"But ye have an unction from the Holy One, and ye know all things."* Here is another apostle who declares that Jesus is, indeed, *"the Holy One."* Putting these passages together, we can see that Christ was truly holy, absolutely holy.

In the Old Testament, it is Jehovah God who is called *"the Holy One."* The prophet Isaiah, no fewer than thirty times, declares Jehovah to be *"the Holy One of Israel."* (See, for example, Isaiah 10:20; 29:19; 43:3.) When Jehovah became flesh and was tabernacled in the Person of Jesus Christ, He was set forth as "the Holy One." The word *holy* means absolutely free from moral defilement or defect. To say that Jesus Christ is "the Holy One" is to say that Jesus Christ *"is light, and in him is no darkness at all"* (1 John 1:5). Christ even said this about Himself: *"I am the light of the world: he that followeth me shall not walk in darkness, but shall have the light of life"* (John 8:12).

The Word Emphasizes Jesus' Holiness

Second, the fact that Jesus Christ was holy—absolutely holy—
is emphasized in the Bible through repetition, one of the ways in
which biblical literature capitalizes on certain points. Many passages tell of Christ's holiness, giving an adequate conception or
impression of the absolute moral purity of Christ. For example, we
read in Hebrews 7:26, *"For such an high priest became us, who is holy,
harmless, undefiled, separate from sinners, and made higher than the
heavens."* Also, we read in Hebrews 9:14, *"How much more shall the
blood of Christ, who through the eternal Spirit offered himself without
spot to God, purge your conscience from dead works to serve the living
God?"* And in 1 Peter 1:19, we read about *"the precious blood of
Christ, as of a lamb without blemish and without spot."*

Here are even more references to Christ's holiness. In 1 John
3:5, we read, *"And ye know that he was manifested to take away our
sins; and in him is no sin,"* and in 2 Corinthians 5:21, *"For he hath
made him to be sin for us, who knew no sin; that we might be made
the righteousness of God in him."* It is put this way in Hebrews 4:15:
*"For we have not an high priest which cannot be touched with the feel-
ing of our infirmities; but was in all points tempted like as we are, yet
without sin."* Finally, in 1 John 3:3, we read, *"And every man that
hath this hope in him purifieth himself, even as he is pure."*

Note how the Holy Spirit uses these inspired authors to
emphasize figures and phrases describing Christ, in order to give
us an adequate impression of the immaculate, absolute, and infinite
holiness of Jesus Christ. We truly do *"behold his glory, the glory as of
the only begotten of the Father, full of grace and truth"* (1 John 1:14).
The dazzling white light that transformed and glorified the face
and very garments of Jesus on Mt. Tabor was only a faint adum-
bration of the moral glory of infinite holiness that shone within
Him. Still, in the face of all this, many people dare to compare
their own holiness with the holiness of Jesus Christ, saying that

they have already attained unto all the fullness there is in Him. When I imagine Christ in His infinite holiness, I wish to do what Isaiah did when he *"saw also the Lord sitting upon a throne, high and lifted up"* (Isaiah 6:1) and heard the seraphim cry, *"Holy, holy, holy, is the* LORD *of hosts: the whole earth is full of his glory"* (verse 3). He covered his face and cried, *"Woe is me! for I am undone; because I am a man of unclean lips, and I dwell in the midst of a people of unclean lips"* (verse 5). I could not but say what Job said when he saw the Lord with his own eyes: *"I abhor myself, and repent in dust and ashes"* (Job 42:6).

How the Holiness of Jesus Christ Manifests Itself

Now let us look at how the holiness of the real Christ, Jesus of Nazareth, manifests itself.

In a Love of Righteousness/a Hatred of Iniquity

The holiness of Jesus Christ manifests itself, in the first place, in a love of righteousness and a hatred of iniquity. Hebrews 1:9 says, *"Thou hast loved righteousness, and hated iniquity; therefore God, even thy God, hath anointed thee with the oil of gladness above thy fellows."* Here, we learn that it is not enough to love righteousness; iniquity must be hated, as well. On the other hand, it is not enough to hate iniquity; righteousness must be loved, as well. There are those who profess to love righteousness but do not seem to hate iniquity. They are strong in applauding right but not equally strong in denouncing evil. There are also those who profess to hate sin but do not seem to love righteousness. They are strong in denouncing evil but not equally strong in applauding right. The holiness of the real Christ, our Lord Jesus, was full-orbed—He loved righteousness and He hated iniquity.

In Deed and Word

Second, the holiness of Jesus Christ manifests itself in both deed and word; negatively, in His never doing wrong or speaking falsehood, and positively, in His always doing right and speaking things that pleased God. Read, for example, 1 Peter 2:22: "[Christ] *did no sin, neither was guile found in his mouth.*" Also read John 8:29: "*And he that sent me is with me: the Father hath not left me alone; for I do always those things that please him.*" Compare Matthew 17:5, "*While he yet spake, behold, a bright cloud overshadowed them: and behold a voice out of the cloud, which said, This is my beloved Son, in whom I am well pleased; hear ye him,*" and John 12:49, "*For I have not spoken of myself; but the Father which sent me, he gave me a com-mandment, what I should say, and what I should speak.*"

There are two things to carefully take note of here. First, notice that the holiness of Christ manifested itself not merely in His deeds but also in His words. Today, many people make great professions of holiness in their actions but are very unholy in their words. Second, note that the holiness of Christ did not merely manifest itself negatively in His not doing or speaking wrong, but also positively in His speaking and doing all that God desired— all that was right to do or speak. A full manifestation of holiness, therefore, does not merely consist in doing nothing wrong but in doing all that is right and saying all that ought to be said. Friends, it is comparatively easy never to say what we ought not to say and never to do what we ought not to do, but the really hard thing is to always do the thing God would be pleased to have us do and always to say the thing, and everything, God would have us say.

In His Victory over Sin

Third, the holiness of Christ manifests in His unfailing vic-tory over sin. This is brought to light in Hebrews 4:15, "*For we have not an high priest which cannot be touched with the feeling of our* infirmities; *but was in all points tempted like as we are, yet without sin.*" The holiness of our Lord was not the mere innocence that resulted from not coming into contact with evil but the holiness that resulted from meeting evil and overcoming it.

In His Uncompromising Perfection

Fourth, the holiness of Jesus Christ manifests itself in demanding absolute perfection from His disciples and refusing to accept any compromise with evil. This is made clear in Matthew 5:48: "*Be ye therefore perfect, even as your Father which is in heaven is perfect.*" The Sermon on the Mount is an illustration of this same thing. Because Jesus Christ was infinitely holy, He could not be satisfied with anything less than perfect holiness in you and me. Some people wish that He had set the standard lower, but I rejoice and glorify God that He set the standard as high as He did. If He had set the standard lower, He would not have been the real Christ— the absolute, holy Christ.

In His Dealings with Sinners

Fifth, the holiness of Jesus Christ manifests itself in His stern and scathing rebuke of sinners. We see this time and time again in the Scriptures. For example, in Matthew 23:13, we read, "*But woe unto you, scribes and Pharisees, hypocrites! For ye shut up the kingdom of heaven against men: for ye neither go in yourselves, neither suffer ye them that are entering to go in.*" In Matthew 16:23, Christ says to Peter, "*Get thee behind me, Satan: thou art an offence unto me: for thou savourest not the things that be of God, but those that be of men.*"

Jesus Christ laid bare the Samaritan woman's sin in a similarly unsparing way in John 4:17–18: "*The woman answered and said, I have no husband. Jesus said unto her, Thou hast well said, I have no husband: for thou hast had five husbands; and he whom thou now hast is not thy husband: in that saidst thou truly.*" We read still sterner words in Matthew 23:33: "*Ye serpents, ye generation of vipers, how can ye escape the damnation of hell?*"

Why did our loving Lord rebuke sin so sternly, so scathingly, so mercilessly? He had to because of who He was, because He was holy, because He was "*light, and in him is no darkness at all.*" Yes, He was "*the meek and lowly Jesus*" (Matthew 11:29), but not the meek and lowly Jesus as He is so often caricatured as, looking upon sin with indulgence and excuse and allowance. No! Never! Sinners He loved, but sin He hated. He rebuked it sternly and scathingly with words that shriveled as if they were in hot fire.

In His Sacrifice

Sixth, the holiness of our Lord Jesus Christ manifests itself in His great sacrifice to save others from the sin He hated so that they could live in the righteousness He loved. We are shown this countless times in the Scriptures. For example, we read in 1 Peter 2:24, "*Who his own self bare our sins in his own body on the tree, that we, being dead to sins, should live unto righteousness: by whose stripes ye were healed.*" Again, in 1 Peter 3:18, we read, "*For Christ also hath once suffered for sins, the just for the unjust, that he might bring us to God, being put to death in the flesh, but quickened by the Spirit.*" Yet again, in 2 Corinthians 5:21, we read, "*He hath made him to be sin for us, who knew no sin; that we might be made the righteousness of God in him.*"

Included here are even more Scriptures of His great sacrifice. A remarkable picture is drawn in Philippians 2:6–8:

[Christ] *being in the form of God, thought it not robbery to be equal with God: but made himself of no reputation, and took upon him the form of a servant, and was made in the likeness of men: and being found in fashion as a man, he humbled*

himself, and became obedient unto death, even the death of
the cross.

The clear meaning of this is that in order to save men from the sin He hated so that they could live in the righteousness He loved, Jesus Christ had to turn His back on equality with God and become a man. He submitted Himself to the lowest disgrace and the most awful suffering a man could endure. Who can fathom holiness such as this? Again, in Galatians 3:13, we read, "*Christ hath redeemed us from the curse of the law, being made a curse for us: for it is written, Cursed is every one that hangeth on a tree.*" A statement of the same magnitude is found in Isaiah's prophetic vision of the coming Christ:

> *But he was wounded for our transgressions, he was bruised for our iniquities: the chastisement of our peace was upon him; and with his stripes we are healed. All we like sheep have gone astray; we have turned every one to his own way; and the LORD hath laid on him the iniquity of us all.*
> (Isaiah 53:5–6)

Here was the crowning manifestation of Christ's holiness. He hated sin so much and loved righteousness so much that He was willing to give up His divine glory and become a man so that others might not sin. He was willing to die as a malefactor, be rejected of man, and be separated from God. He was willing to sacrifice everything to free all of creation from sin.

Men look at the cross and say that they see the love of God and the love of Christ. Yes, they are wonderfully set forth there. But ask the Holy Spirit to reveal something more—the holiness of Christ's atoning death. He so hated sin and so loved righteousness that He made the most matchless, marvelous, unfathomable sacrifice in order to save men and women from an eternity of sin!

In Future Punishment of Evildoers

Seventh, the holiness of Jesus Christ will, in the future, manifest itself in the awful, irrevocable punishment of those who refuse to be separated from their sin. We see this time and time again in the Scriptures. For example, here are the awful words of the Lord in Matthew 25:31–32, 41:

> When the Son of man shall come in his glory, and all the holy angels with him, then shall he sit upon the throne of his glory: and before him shall be gathered all nations: and he shall separate them one from another, as a shepherd divideth his sheep from the goats....Then shall he say also unto them on the left hand, Depart from me, ye cursed, into everlasting fire, prepared for the devil and his angels.

We read again in 2 Thessalonians 1:7–9:

> And to you who are troubled rest with us, when the Lord Jesus shall be revealed from heaven with his mighty angels, in flaming fire taking vengeance on them that know not God, and that obey not the gospel of our Lord Jesus Christ: who shall be punished with everlasting destruction from the presence of the Lord, and from the glory of his power.

Why must men who do not receive the Savior perish forever? Because the real Christ is holy. He died to save men from the sin He hates so that they might live in the righteousness He loves. He was willing to give up everything to accomplish that. Language fails to describe the depth and magnitude of His sacrifice. If men thus refuse to accept this sacrifice and to confess their sin, Christ leaves them to the paths they have chosen and the doom that accompanies them. Men talk a lot about God's holiness and Jesus' love, but the real Jesus is just as holy as God, and God is just as loving as Jesus. In this case and in all others, Jesus and the Father are one.

Jesus is Holy First and Foremost

Let us remember, then, when we try to picture the real Christ, that He is first of all holy. Until we have an adequate understanding of His holiness, we cannot have an adequate understanding of His love.

And the Word was made flesh, and dwelt among us, (and we beheld his glory, the glory as of the only begotten of the Father,) full of grace and truth. (John 1:14)

2

HIS LOVE
FOR THE FATHER

*"But that the world may know that I love the Father; and as
the Father gave me commandment, even so I do."*
—John 14:31

Now we continue on with the subject of the real Christ, the
Christ of God's own appointment and actual historical fact,
as distinguished from the "Christ" of man's dreams and fancies
and imaginings. We will talk of the Christ, whose picture God
Himself has drawn in the Bible as distinguished from the "Christ"
of Christian Science, Theosophy, Unitarianism, and other forms
of fiction.

In the last chapter, I addressed one special feature that God
has drawn of Christ—His holiness. Now we will look at another
feature of the Holy One—His love for the Father.

In the book of John, the Lord Jesus shares that the one thing
He wished the world to know about Him was that He loved the

Father. *"But that the world may know that I love the Father; and as the Father gave me commandment, even so I do"* (John 14:31). In these days, we often speak and think of love as it is with our fellow man, an altruism of some sort. Modern thought is so exclusively occupied with man that it scarcely enters our minds that God should be the supreme object of our love. Our obligation to love God is immeasurably greater than our obligation to love our fellow man. Yet most people echo the sentiment of the gifted poet who exalted the one who was "a lover of his fellow man" above the one who loved God. Our Lord Jesus loved His fellow man as no other human being has ever loved his fellow man. Far deeper than His love to his fellow man, however—and the very foundation for this love—was His love for the Father. This was also the one thing that He wished the world knew about Him—that He loved the Father. So it should be with us.

It is greatly important to love our fellow man. It is true that loving our fellow man is one of the greatest solutions to our social problems, industrial problems, political problems, and international problems. No merely external League of Nations will ever set things straight. No external social adjustment will set things straight. No triumph of universal democracy will set things straight. Only love in the heart for our fellow man will set things straight. If love ruled in the hearts of capitalists and laborers, in the hearts of Americans, Englishmen, Italians, Slovaks, Germans, Japanese, Chinese, and all other ethnicities, then many of our social, industrial, and international problems would be settled within a few days.

No philosopher or number of philosophers could ever foster universal justice and equality and peace in our societies while selfishness rules in the hearts of men. As important as love for our fellow man is, however, our love for God is immeasurably more important. God is infinite, man is finite; and we would do well to remember that no number of finites can ever equal infinity. The whole human race put together—all of the billions who are now living and all of the billions who have lived in the past—are as the *"small dust of the balance"* (Isaiah 40:15) compared with the one infinite God. If we should render our full measure of love to the whole human race and fail to love the infinite God as we ought, we have failed. It was because Christ loved the Father that He loved His fellow man. Likewise, we will never love our fellow man in reality until we love the Father. John wrote, *"We love him, because he first loved us"* (1 John 4:19). When we start to believe Christ's love, then we begin to love God and so begin to love our fellow man. Read what John writes in 1 John 4:11: *"Beloved, if God so loved us, we also ought to love one another."*

Scriptural Manifestations of Christ's Love for the Father

Now we will take a look at the love that Jesus Christ had for the Father. When we look at Scripture, we find that there were many ways in which Christ's love for the Father manifested itself.

In His Obedience

First, the love of our Lord Jesus for the Father manifested itself in His obedience to the Father's command. Jesus said, *"But that the world may know that I love the Father; and as the Father gave me commandment, even so I do"* (John 14:31). The same thought is found in John 15:10: *"If ye keep my commandments, ye shall abide in my love; even as I have kept my Father's commandments, and abide in his love."*

Christ Jesus' love for the Father was true. He not only loved Him in word and tongue but also *"in deed and in truth"* (1 John 3:18). Because of this, His ear was ever listening for God's instruction, and He was quick to obey it. So it is with everyone who really loves God. Many of us talk about loving God, but our ears are not listening for His instructions. Neither are we quick to obey His commands when we do hear them.

It was for the sole purpose—a glad and not reluctant purpose—of obeying God and doing His Father's will that Jesus turned His back on heaven's glory and entered into the shame and agony of earth. He said in John 6:38, *"For I came down from heaven, not to do mine own will, but the will of him that sent me."* His love for the Father faltered not at forsaking the glory of heaven for the shame of earth, because He knew it was the Father's will. We might do well to stop and think about this love for a while. How do our lives measure up to God's standard—Christ Jesus?

Jesus came into this world to fulfill the Father's plan, and He never faltered at obeying His commands—even when it came to dying on a cross. *"And being found in fashion as a man, he humbled himself, and became obedient unto death, even the death of the cross"* (Philippians 2:8). Jesus Christ's death was entirely voluntary. Some say that His death was an unavoidable incident of His fidelity to duty, but God tells us in His Word that it was the purpose for which He came into the world and the goal toward which He deliberately walked. Jesus Himself says in John 10:17–18, *"Therefore doth my Father love me, because I lay down my life, that I might take it again. No man taketh it from me, but I lay it down of myself. I have power to lay it down, and I have power to take it again. This commandment have I received of my Father."*

We read in Luke 9:51 of His last journey to Jerusalem, where the cross awaited Him: *"And it came to pass, when the time was come that he should be received up, he stedfastly set his face to go to Jerusalem."* This was not the only journey for which He had steadfastly set His face; He did the same when He first took upon Himself the nature of man. As the Jews stood beside Lazarus' tomb and beheld Jesus weeping, they said, *"Behold how he loved him!"* (John 11:36). Today, we stand beside the cross as we behold Jesus bleeding, suffering, and dying, and say together, "Behold, how He loved the Father."

In His Observance of the Word

Second, the love of Jesus Christ for the Father manifested itself in His careful keeping of His Father's Word. We read His own words in John 8:55: *"Yet ye have not known him; but I know him: and if I should say, I know him not, I shall be a liar like unto you: but I know him, and keep his saying."* The word that is translated here as *"keep"* means "to attend to carefully" and "to guard." To keep God's Word means more than to obey His commandments. A man may obey commandments without a hearty love for them. But we guard that which we think of as a precious treasure. This is how the Lord Jesus regarded the words of God. Christ guarded His Father's Word as other men guard their gold and jewels. The esteem He had for the Word was a peculiar mark of His love for the Father.

Oh, how many there are today who profess to love God but still need to learn this lesson. They do not jealously and tenaciously guard and hold fast to God's Word. They are quite willing to give up parts of it that the first glib talker—who claims to be an exponent of the most recent German scholarship—says are not authentic and must go. Look at Professor Kent's infamous "Shorter Bible," in which he unhesitatingly cuts out what God has revealed about Christ's death in Romans 3, just because he does not want to offend anyone. He surrenders God's truth in order to keep peace! What is the fundamental error in these men? A lack of a deep and genuine love for the Father, such as Jesus Christ had. If they had really loved the Father, they would have kept His Word. They would have held on to it regardless of who was displeased. Heed again the words of the real Christ: *"Yet ye have not* known him; but I know him: and if I should say, I know him not, I shall be a liar like unto you: but I know him, and keep his saying" (John 8:55).

In His Submission

Third, the love of Jesus Christ for the Father was manifested in His unwavering submission to the Father's will, even when that will required that from which He shrank in heartbreaking anguish. We see this in the Lord's words in the garden of Gethsemane:

> *And he went a little farther, and fell on his face, and prayed, saying, O my Father, if it be possible, let this cup pass from me: nevertheless not as I will, but as thou wilt....He went away again the second time, and prayed, saying, O my Father, if this cup may not pass away from me, except I drink it, thy will be done.* (Matthew 26:39, 42)

No man who ever lived on this earth recoiled from death like our Lord Jesus did, for no other man was as full of life as He. He contemplated death with heartbreaking agony. In view of His coming death, His soul was "*exceeding sorrowful, even unto death*" (Matthew 26:38); but, though He recoiled from it, He faced it gladly because it was the Father's will. Consider again what He says: "*O my Father, if it be possible, let this cup pass from me: nevertheless not as I will, but as thou wilt.*" Can we, too, submit to our Lord's will, even in suffering? We must be ready to, for He Himself has said, "*If any man will come after me, let him deny himself, and take up his cross, and follow me*" (Matthew 16:24).

In His Delight in God's Will

Fourth, the love of Jesus Christ for the Father manifested itself in the delight He found in doing God's will. He said, "*I delight to do thy will, O my God: yea, thy law is within my heart"* (Psalm 40:8). The Father's will in which Christ delighted was His own sacrificial death on the cross. Not only do we see Christ submitting to the Father's will, but we actually see Him delighting in it. Do you have a love for God like that? Do you love Him so much that you delight in His will simply because it is His will—even if that means crucifixion for you? Oh, here lies the secret of a blessedness and a joy that nothing or no one could ever destroy.

Even in childhood, Jesus delighted in the Father's will. Take a look at Luke chapter 2. When Mary finds Christ after searching for three days, she says to Him, *"Son, why hast thou thus dealt with us? Behold, thy father and I have sought thee sorrowing"* (Luke 2:48), to which He replied, *"How is it that ye sought me? wist ye not that I must be about my Father's business ["in my Father's house"* RV]*?" (2:49). The literal translation would read, "Knew ye not that I must be in the things of My Father?" We see here that even in childhood, Jesus realized that His delight was in the things of God and in the will of God.

Throughout the course of His life on earth, Jesus found that doing His Father's will was His very meat and drink, His sustenance, His satisfaction, and His joy. We have a striking illustration of this in the fourth chapter of John. Jesus and the disciples arrive at the well of Samaria in the evening. Jesus goes to the well, for He is weary, thirsty, and hungry. His disciples go into Sychar to find Him some food, for He is too tired to accompany them into town. Soon after, Jesus begins talking with a Samaritan woman who shows up at the well. He offers her living water—water that will bring her eternal life so that she will never thirst again. As He talks with the woman, the disciples return with the food, saying, *"Master, eat"* (John 4:31). But He replies, *"I have meat to eat that ye know not of"* (verse 32). Then the disciples say one to another, *"Hath any man brought him ought to eat?"* (verse 33). And Jesus says,

"*My meat is to do the will of him that sent me, and to finish his work*" (verse 34). He was so wrapped up in the joy of doing His Father's will that He had forgotten about His physical hunger and weariness. Indeed, doing His Father's will was His very meat and drink, His sustenance, His satisfaction, His joy.

In His Desire to Please God

Fifth, the love of Jesus Christ to the Father manifested itself in His desire to do what pleased the Father. He says in John 8:29, "*He that sent me is with me: the Father hath not left me alone; for I do always those things that please him.*" Jesus, the Son of God, so loved the Father that He made it His earnest study to find out what pleased Him and then always did it. This is far more than obedience to explicit commandments. A son may do whatever a father bids him, but a more loyal, loving son will not wait to be bidden. To know what pleased the Father was Jesus Christ's constant study; to do the things that pleased the Father was His unvarying practice. There is a lesson here that we can all learn from. Many of us think that if we do the things God commands us to do and leave undone the things that God specifically commands us not to do, we will have done all that God's love requires of us. Oh, not at all. Love requires more than that. The love of God in our hearts will irresistibly impel us to make it our earnest and constant study to know what pleases the Father and to do it without being told.

How this would simplify our lives! How many of our problems would be solved if we acted on this principle? Shall I go to the theatre? Shall I play cards? Shall I patronize the movies? Shall I smoke? Shall I do this, that, and the other thing? The answer to all these questions can be found in asking oneself, "Will it bring more joy to God for me to do these things than for me not to do them?" If so, do them; if not, do not do them. Is that the principle upon which you act every day? What's that? No? Then you do not love God. Learn how to love God from Christ's example. From this time on, make it the principle of your life to find out what pleases God and to do that every time.

In His Seeking Out the Father's Will

Sixth, the love of Jesus Christ for the Father manifested itself in His seeking out the Father's will. This we see in John 5:30: "*I can of mine own self do nothing: as I hear, I judge: and my judgment is just; because I seek not mine own will, but the will of the Father which hath sent me.*" The word from the original text that is translated "*seek*" in this verse means "to seek in order to find." It is also used in Matthew 13:45 about the man seeking pearls. The thought is that accomplishing the Father's will was the object of Christ's pursuit. As other men hunted for jewels, gold, pleasure, honor, or to fulfill their own will, Christ sought to accomplish His Father's will. What are you seeking? Money? Pleasure? Honor? Or are you seeking for God's will to be done in your life?

In His Acceptance of the Father's Testimony and Glory

Seventh, the love of the real Christ—Christ Jesus—for the Father manifested itself in His acceptance of the Father's testimony and glory. He made this clear when He said, "*But I receive not testimony from man: but these things I say, that ye might be saved....I receive not honour from men*" (John 5:34, 41). Jesus Christ loved the Father so much that He found all His needs and desires satisfied in Him. For this reason, He sought no praise and accepted no praise from others. It was the Father's testimony, the Father's approval, and the Father's praise that He desired and accepted. What a lesson for you and me. How eagerly and persistently we seek admiration and praise from men. How gladly we accept it when it comes. How we treasure the fine things that are said about us in newspapers or books. Let us have done with it! Let us love God so completely that His approval is all that we care about and all that we will accept.

In His Desire to Finish His Work

Eighth, the love of Jesus Christ for the Father manifested itself in His desire to finish the work that the Father had given Him to do. We see this desire plainly in John 17:4: *"I have glorified thee on the earth: I have finished the work which thou gavest me to do."*

Jesus Christ loved the Father and desired nothing more than to accomplish the work that He had assigned to Him, and so He did. When was this work completed? It was completed on the cross when He cried, *"It is finished"* (John 19:30). We have already seen that Jesus shrank from the cross in unutterable agony. Still, He marched to the cross because it was the only place where He could accomplish and complete the Father's will for His life. It was love for God the Father (before love for you and me) that brought our Lord Jesus to Calvary. We speak of God the Father loving men in Christ Jesus, which is true, but it is also true that Christ's sacrifice for men finds its origin in obedience to the will of the Father. Has God given you some work to do? Indeed, He has. He has work for each one of us to do. And does the completion of that work—the perfect consummation of it—lead to some Gethsemane or Calvary? This is very likely. Let us march on to Calvary, then, without hesitation, no matter how much our hearts recoil from the agony that awaits us there.

In His Desire to Glorify the Father

Ninth, the love of Jesus Christ for the Father manifested itself in His desire for God to receive glory. There are many verses that establish this truth. In the verse just quoted above, we see that Christ said, *"I have glorified thee on the earth"* (John 17:4). He also said, *"Father, the hour is come; glorify thy Son, that thy Son also may glorify thee"* (John 17:1). Furthermore, we learn that *"he that speaketh of himself seeketh his own glory: but he that seeketh his glory that sent him, the same is true, and no unrighteousness is in him"* (John 7:18).

The Father's glory was Jesus Christ's first and greatest ambition, the consuming passion of His life. It was for the Father's glory that He planned, prayed, lived, acted, suffered, and died. Jesus taught that the first and greatest commandment was, *"Thou shalt love the Lord thy God with all thy heart, and with all thy soul, and with all thy mind"* (Matthew 22:37). His own life is the supreme manifestation of this law. Is God's glory the supreme thing you are seeking? Have you utterly lost sight of your own glory, your own profit, your own ease, your own pleasure, your own everything? Remember, *"He that saith he abideth in him ought himself also so to walk, even as he walked"* (1 John 2:6).

3

HIS LOVE FOR MEN

"Unto him that loved us, and washed us from our sins in his own blood."
—Revelation 1:5

"For ye know the grace of our Lord Jesus Christ, that, though he was rich, yet for your sakes he became poor, that ye through his poverty might be rich."
—2 Corinthians 8:9

We continue on with the subject of the real Christ, the Christ of God's own appointment and actual historical fact, as distinguished from the Christ of man's dreams and fancies and imaginings. We are still talking about the Christ whose picture God Himself has drawn in the Bible, as distinguished from the "Christ" of Christian Science, Theosophy, Unitarianism, Spiritualism, and other forms of fiction. We have looked at His holiness and His love for the Father. Now we will consider a third feature of the picture, as seen in the verses listed above—namely, the love of Christ for His fellow man.

These are wonderful texts. Hopefully, by the end of this study, they will mean more to you than they have ever meant before. We have already considered how our Lord Jesus loved His fellow man as no other man has ever loved his fellow man. Nevertheless, the very foundation of His love for His fellow man was and is His love for Christ. His love for the Father is far higher than His love for His fellow man. So it should be with us. Our love for the Father should be deeper—far deeper—and higher than our love for our fellow man. It should be the very foundation of our love for others!

Further, God tells us in His Word that Jesus' love for His fellow man is an example for us to follow. As John put it in 1 John 3:16, *"Hereby perceive we the love of God, because he laid down his life for us: and we ought to lay down our lives for the brethren."*

What we have discovered in the picture of Christ's love for His fellow man, as pictured in God's Word, can be broken down into two sections: who among men Jesus loved and how the love of Christ for men manifested itself.

Who Among Men Jesus Loved

The Church

First of all, Jesus Christ loved the church. This we find explicitly stated in Ephesians 5:25: *"Husbands, love your wives, even as Christ also loved the church, and gave himself for it."* Jesus Christ, as we shall see later on, loves individual men; the particular object of His love, however, is the church. The church is loved by Christ in a particular sense and in a peculiar way. A philanthropist may love all mankind, and yet, if he is a true man, he will love his own wife in a peculiar way, as he loves no other woman. So Christ has peculiar love for the church, His bride. We must take note of the passages we study in the Bible that speak of Christ's love—whether they refer to His love in general, as in His love for all mankind, or His love in particular, as in His love for the church—His body and bride.

Who is meant by the "church"? Not, of course, any particular denomination or the church as an external organization. The "church" that is referred to in the New Testament refers is a group of people who are "called out" of the present dispensation; that is to say, all those who accept Jesus Christ as their personal Savior, surrender to Him as their Lord and Master, and confess Him as such before the world, living in obedience to His will.

Christ's peculiar love for His church is beautifully set forth in John 13:1: *"Now before the feast of the passover, when Jesus knew that his hour was come that he should depart out of this world unto the Father, having loved his own which were in the world, he loved them unto the end."* This body of people is spoken of as *"his own."* Why Christ calls the church His own is made clear in the following passage:

> *As thou hast given him power over all flesh, that he should give eternal life to as many as thou hast given him....I pray for them: I pray not for the world, but for them which thou hast given me; for they are thine....While I was with them in the world, I kept them in thy name: those that thou gavest me I have kept, and none of them is lost, but the son of perdition; that the scripture might be fulfilled.* (John 17:2, 9, 12)

It is evident here that Jesus Christ's "own" are those whom God the Father has given unto Him. That is to say, there is a body of people out of the human race whom God has given unto

Jesus Christ as His own peculiar property. The proof that anyone belongs to this elect company is that he comes to Christ, as we read in John 6:37: *"All that the Father giveth me shall come to me; and him that cometh to me I will in no wise cast out."* This highly favored company, which was given unto Christ by the Father, is the object of Christ's special love. He ministers in a special way to those in the church (see John 13:1) and guards them so they do not perish (see John 17:12). He says of them, *"Of them which thou gavest me have I lost none"* (John 18:9).

Individual Believers

Second, Jesus Christ not only loves the church as a body, but He also loves each individual member in a peculiar way. One of the greatest examples of this love is found in Galatians 2:20 when Paul talks about how Christ loves him: *"I am crucified with Christ: nevertheless I live; yet not I, but Christ liveth in me: and the life which I now live in the flesh I live by the faith of the Son of God, who loved me, and gave himself for me."*

Those Who Love God and Keep His Commandments

Third, Jesus Christ had an altogether peculiar and particular love for those who loved Him and showed their love to Him by keeping His commandments. He said in John 14:21, *"He that hath my commandments, and keepeth them, he it is that loveth me: and he that loveth me shall be loved of my Father, and I will love him, and will manifest myself to him."*

He expressed much the same thought in Mark 3:35: *"For whosoever shall do the will of God, the same is my brother, and my sister, and mother."* Whosoever does the will of God stands in a much closer kinship with Christ as a "brother, sister, and mother." A man may love all men and still have a peculiar love for his brother, his sister, and especially his mother. Here, our Lord tells us that His love for those who do the will of God is equivalent to combining all these great loves into one.

Individuals

Fourth, Jesus loved each individual in a special way. In John 19:26, John is spoken of as *"the disciple…whom he [Jesus] loved."* We also read in John 11:5 that *"Jesus loved Martha, and her sister, and Lazarus."* While Jesus loves all men with infinite love, while He has a peculiar love for His church, while He has an individual love for each member of His body, while He has a still more special love for those who keep His commandments and do His Father's will, He takes more delight in those whose hearts are more open to Him in faith and love.

Sinners

Fifth, Jesus Christ loved sinners—the lost, the ungodly, the utterly vile. We see this time and time again in the picture God has drawn of Christ in the Bible. For example, Christ said, *"I am not come to call the righteous, but sinners"* (Matthew 9:13), and *"The Son of man is come to seek and to save that which was lost"* (Luke 19:10). Paul wrote, *"For when we were yet without strength, in due time Christ died for the ungodly.…But God commendeth his love toward us, in that, while we were yet sinners, Christ died for us"* (Romans 5:6, 8). Jesus Christ loves the vilest sinner as truly as He loves the purest saint, but He does not love the vilest sinner in the same way He loves the purest saint. His love for the sinner is one thing; His love for the obedient disciple is quite another. He has pity toward one and pleasure for the other. There is an attraction in both cases. In the one case, it is the attraction to compassion; in the other, it is the attraction to moral beauty, with appreciation and delight. Christ pities the sinner; He delights in the saint. He loves them both. In the parable of the lost sheep, we see that to Jesus Christ, the attraction of need was greater than the attraction of moral beauty. (See Luke 15:3–7.)

Among the sinners whom Jesus loved were His bitterest and cruelest enemies. On the cross, He forgot His own agonies in His concern for those who had nailed Him to the cross. In His last moments, He cried, *"Father, forgive them; for they know not what they do"* (Luke 23:34). Here is a lesson we can all learn from our Lord's example.

How the Love of Christ for Men Manifested Itself

We will now look more closely at the picture God has drawn of the real Christ in the Bible and see how His love for men manifested itself. I am staggered at the wealth of material God presents us with on this topic in the Word. During a careful study of this subject years ago, I found that there were no fewer than thirty separate and distinct ways in which the love of Jesus Christ for men manifested itself. We will look at some of the most striking examples.

In His Willingness to Become Poor to Make Us Rich

First, the love of Jesus Christ for men manifested itself in His willingness to become poor so that we might be rich. Second Corinthians 8:9 says, *"For ye know the grace of our Lord Jesus Christ, that, though he was rich, yet for your sakes he became poor, that ye through his poverty might be rich.*" As we can see in Philippians 2:6–8, He renounced many riches:

> [Jesus], *being in the form of God, thought it not robbery to be equal with God: but made himself of no reputation, and took upon him the form of a servant, and was made in the likeness of men: and being found in fashion as a man, he humbled himself, and became obedient unto death, even the death of the cross.*

In Romans 8:16–17, we see the great riches that we may receive because of His willingness to become poor: "*The Spirit itself beareth witness with our spirit, that we are the children of God: and if children, then heirs; heirs of God, and joint-heirs with Christ; if so be that we suffer with him, that we may be also glorified together.*" We might do well to stop here and ponder and wonder and admire and adore our wondrous Lord. Before we move on, let me say that even in this wondrous sacrifice of His, He has left an example for us to follow. First John 2:6 says, "*He that saith he abideth in him ought himself also so to walk, even as he walked.*"

In His Willingness to Give Himself Up For Us

Second, the love of Jesus Christ for men manifested itself in His willingness to give Himself up for us. We see this in Galatians 2:20: "*The Son of God, who loved me…gave himself for me.*" He had a self-sacrificing love. Not only did He sacrifice His life for us; He sacrificed Himself for us. Even though it was a crowning sacrifice, Christ's death on the cross was not His only sacrifice for us. His whole life—from the manger to the cross—was a sacrifice. The fact that He became a man was a sacrifice of immeasurable greatness and meaning, in and of itself.

These sacrifices are more than adequate a reason for us to lay down our lives for Christ. They also provide an example for us to follow. God Himself tells us so. In Ephesians 5:2, His Word says, *"Walk in love, as Christ also hath loved us, and hath given himself for us an offering and a sacrifice to God for a sweetsmelling savour."* We also read in 1 John 3:16, in words that can neither be misunderstood nor evaded, *"Hereby perceive we the love of God, because he laid down his life for us: and we ought to lay down our lives for the brethren."*

In His Willingness to Forgive Repentant Sinners

Third, the love of Jesus Christ for the vilest sinners manifested itself in His willingness to forgive them when they repented of their sin and believed in Him. The picture God draws of Christ in the Bible successfully illustrates this. Take, for instance, the example we find in Luke 7 of the woman who poured ointment over Christ's feet. The woman, who was a notorious sinner, drew near Him as He reclined at the table, wet His feet with her tears, and wiped them with her hair. Simon and the other guests were shocked that He would allow such a sinful woman to even touch Him. In response, Jesus turned to the woman and said, *"Thy faith hath saved thee; go in peace"* (Luke 7:50). We are specifically told to imitate Jesus' kindness and mercy—so clearly set forth in this passage—to others who have wronged us. Ephesians 4:32 says, *"Be ye kind one to another, tenderhearted, forgiving one another, even as God for Christ's sake hath forgiven you."*

In His Chastening

Fourth, the love of Jesus Christ for men manifested itself in His rebuking and chastening of them when they sinned in order to bring them to repentance. Speaking from the glory, Jesus Christ says in Revelation 3:19, *"As many as I love, I rebuke and chasten: be zealous therefore, and repent."* We often wrongly believe a one-sided picture of Jesus Christ. We are eager to believe His readiness to forgive sinners—even the vilestest of sinners—but are hesitant to believe that He makes the impenitent sinner suffer in order to bring him to repentance. Such a Christ is not the real Christ. It is not the Christ of actual fact. It is not the Christ God Himself has pictured for us in His Word.

In His Patience with Doubters

Fifth, the love of Christ toward skeptics was manifested in His patience in dealing with unreasonable, inexcusable, and stubborn doubts. There are various illustrations of this in the Bible. One of the most striking illustrations is found in the story of doubting Thomas. Thomas was not among the disciples who saw the risen Christ on the night of the resurrection. When they told him, *"We have seen the Lord,"* Thomas stubbornly replied, *"Except I shall see in his hands the print of the nails, and put my finger into the print of the nails, and thrust my hand into his side, I will not believe"* (John 20:25). A week from that night, the next Lord's Day, Christ appeared to all of the disciples as they were gathered together and said, *"Peace be unto you"* (John 20:26). Then He turned to Thomas, the stubborn doubter, and gently said, *"Reach hither thy finger, and behold my hands; and reach hither thy hand, and thrust it into my side: and be not faithless, but believing"* (John 20:27). Thomas' doubt vanished. He fell to his knees before the Lord, looked up into His face, and cried, *"My Lord and my God"* (John 20:28). There is a lesson all of us can learn from this story. It is easy to grow impatient with one who doubts, who is stubborn and unreasonable in his doubt, but we are to have patience with him, like our Lord had with Thomas.

In His Patience with Sinners

Sixth, the love of Jesus Christ for weak disciples manifested itself in His patience and tender dealing with their lapse into grievous sin and awful apostasy. The case we will examine here is the story of Peter's denial of Christ. After His resurrection, Christ gives a certain message to the women who visit the tomb to deliver to the disciples. He tells them, *"But go your way, tell his disciples and Peter that he goeth before you into Galilee: there shall ye see him, as he said unto you"* (Mark 16:7). Oh, how wondrously tender was that *"and Peter."* Why so? Was he not a disciple? Yes, he was the leader of the apostolic company. But he had denied his Lord three times and felt the shame and dread of his awful act.

If Christ had said only, "Tell his disciples," Peter could have easily replied, "Yes, I was a disciple, but I am no longer. I denied my Lord with oaths and curses. He doesn't mean me." Knowing this, our loving Lord told the messengers, "Go and tell My disciples, and be sure you tell poor, discouraged, brokenhearted Peter." Herein lies a message for us. We are often ready to rebuke with harsh words those who are weak, and, in so doing, discourage them. But our Lord shows us that when professed Christians prove weak, when they fail in the hour of testing, we are to follow in the footsteps of our Lord and deal with them patiently and tenderly, no matter how grievous their lapse into sin might have been. We do all of this to bring them back into the fold and to win them back for Christ.

In His Willingness to Serve

Seventh, the love of Christ for His disciples manifested itself in His willingness to perform the lowliest and most menial acts of service for them. Perhaps one of the most beautiful acts of service our Christ performs for the disciples is described in John 13:1–5:

Now before the feast of the passover, when Jesus knew that his hour was come that he should depart out of this world unto the

Father, having loved his own which were in the world, he loved them unto the end. And supper being ended, the devil having now put into the heart of Judas Iscariot, Simon's son, to betray him; Jesus knowing that the Father had given all things into his hands, and that he was come from God, and went to God; he riseth from supper, and laid aside his garments; and took a towel, and girded himself. After that he poureth water into a basin, and began to wash the disciples' feet, and to wipe them with the towel wherewith he was girded.

What a sight! What a sight! The Lord of glory washed the dirty feet of those mutually jealous disciples. We might take a few moments to dwell on the significance of this wonderful scene. More than anything, though, what Jesus did needs our imitation more than our comments. The Lord clearly says that this act was an example for us to follow. His words are, *"For I have given you an example, that ye should do as I have done to you"* (John 13:15).

In His Leaving the Father and Cleaving to the Church

Eighth, the love of Jesus Christ for the church was manifested in His willingness to leave the Father in order to cleave to the church. His desire was to become one with it. This stupendous fact is made clear in Ephesians 5:31–32: *"For this cause shall a man leave his father and mother, and shall be joined unto his wife, and they two shall be one flesh. This is a great mystery: but I speak concerning Christ and the church."* Some are hesitant to interpret these words, but God has put them into His Word so that we might understand them and mediate upon them.

Therefore, we will look at them in greater depth. The idea of marriage was designed in the likeness of Christ's covenant with the church—His bride. Taking a step back, we see that God the Father was the object of the eternal love of Christ. In the eternity behind us, before the world was formed, God the Father loved God the Son, and God the Son loved God the Father. Their whole being was wrapped up in one another. The tendrils of the love of Christ had wrapped themselves around the one object of His eternal love, the Father, with an infinitude of love that we cannot begin to imagine. Then, God created men to share in this love. It was not long, however, before man sinned and was separated from God. Out of all mankind, God gave to His Son an elect group of people with whom to fellowship. The plan was for them to believe Him and become His bride. But they, too, failed like all the others. So, the eternal Son tore Himself away from the Father to come to the sin-cursed world to save His bride and bring her back into communion with Him. It is no wonder that Paul says, *"This is a great mystery."*

In His Preparing a Place for Us

Ninth, the love of Jesus Christ for His disciples manifested itself in His leaving from earth to go and prepare a place for us. In John 14:2, Jesus said, *"In my Father's house are many mansions: if it were not so, I would have told you. I go to prepare a place for you."* It was love for the church that brought Christ down to the earth, and it was love for the church that took Him away from the earth. It was love for the church that made Him leave the Father, win us for Himself, and die to secure our pardon. It was also love for the church that led Him to leave the earth again. He went to prepare an eternal home for us in heaven!

In His Promise to Return

In the tenth place, the love of Jesus Christ for His church will manifest itself in His return to bring us into Himself. We will no longer have to be separated from our Lord and Savior!

Christ said, *"If I go and prepare a place for you, I will come again, and receive you unto myself; that where I am, there ye may be also"* (John 14:3). Oh, how He loves us! He left us out of love for us. He left us for our own good. Heaven is still not complete in that Christ still waits for us to join Him. He loves us that much. Even more so, earth ought to be an incomplete, lonesome place for us without our Lord and Christ—our heavenly Bridegroom. Despite the beauty of our homes, how many our comforts, how numerous and excellent our friends, how noble and satisfying our children, how lovely our wives or husbands, earth ought to be a lonesome place for us because we are separated from Christ. Is earth a lonesome place for you without the Lord Jesus? Are you longing for His return? Does your heart keep crying, *"Even so, come, Lord Jesus"* (Revelation 22:20)? Are you even willing, if He must tarry, to lay aside your mortal body and *"be absent from the body, and to be present with the Lord"* (2 Corinthians 5:8)? Are you saying from the depth of your heart, along with Paul, that you have *"a desire to depart, and to be with Christ; which is far better"* (Philippians 1:23)?

There is a wonderful tenderness in the words of our Christ in this verse: *"I will come again, and receive you unto myself"* (John 14:3). Note the words *"unto myself."* He does not merely say "into My home" or "into companionship with Me" but *"unto myself."* It is as if He longs for us to press into His very soul. Godet's comment on these words is worth repeating: "He presses Him to His heart, so to speak, while bearing Him away. There is an infinite tenderness in these last words. It is for Himself that He seems to rejoice in and look to this moment which will put an end to all separation."

Last summer, I entered a room in a little mission station in China many miles off the beaten track, in which a native pastor once lived. The room was plainly furnished, with only one thing adorning the walls: the words "Come quickly, Lord Jesus."

4

HIS LOVE FOR SOULS

"And the multitude cometh together again, so that they could not so much as eat bread. And when his friends heard of it, they went out to lay hold on him: for they said, He is beside himself."
—Mark 3:20–21

"He that saith he abideth in him ought himself also so to walk, even as he walked."
—1 John 2:6

I have been sharing, under the Holy Spirit's guidance, about the picture God has given in His Word of the real Christ, the Christ of God's own appointment and actual historical fact, as distinguished from the "Christ" of man's dreams and fancies and imaginings. We have learned about His holiness, His love for the Father, and His love for men. Now we will look at the fourth feature of that divinely drawn picture—the love of Jesus Christ for souls.

We shall explore the above verses to help us understand Christ's love for individual souls, in hopes that this study will awaken in us the same love for souls. Oh, how I wish it will! How much it would mean for this city, how much it would mean for this whole country, how much it would mean for this world.

Biblical Illustrations of Jesus' Love for Souls

His Reason for Coming to Earth

First, the love of Jesus Christ for souls is seen in the reason for which He came into this world. He explains this reason in Luke 19:10: *"For the Son of man is come to seek and to save that which was lost."* Seeking and saving the lost was the focus of Christ's earthly mission. He did not come into this world to accumulate wealth or to gain a kingdom. He left behind far greater glories than what this world had to offer. He came for just one purpose—to seek and save the lost. Lost men were more valuable in His sight than all of earth's wealth and glory. Yes, they were even more valuable than heaven's wealth and glory. Nothing was more valuable than a lost soul. Christ is not merely talking about the soul of some great and wise person but the soul of the seemingly most insignificant person, as well. He is talking about the soul of the most foolish and unlearned, the soul of the vilest and most wretched; not only the soul of the philosopher and saint, but also the soul of the savage and the outcast. Each soul has immeasurable value in His sight.

On a Sunday night years ago, I was walking up Waterloo Road in London. The street was full of light. The public houses were filled with people, the stages crowded with many drunken men and women. I came to a dark spot in the road and saw a donkey cart backed up against the curb. Two young men were casting what looked like a filthy, stuffed bag into the donkey cart. I stepped nearer to see what they were doing. Much to my surprise, it was a drunken, besotted, unconscious woman—perhaps fifty years of age—whom they were throwing into the cart. It seemed to me that she was a mother. As I shrank back in horror and disgust, the thought came to my mind: *God loves that woman as truly as He loves you.* This is true. The soul of the most disgusting creature is more valuable than all of the precious gems on the earth. Never forget that Christ *"came to seek and to save that which was lost"* (Luke 19:10).

Some years later, as I was walking through the streets of Benares, India, I saw a fakir—a so-called holy man—sitting almost naked in a cage and staring straight ahead, trying not to blink his eyes or take notice of the people gazing at him. His hair and his body were covered with ashes, a perfect representation of the Buddhist conception of holiness and blessedness. It was a more nauseating sight than the drunken woman I had seen in London, but, as I turned away in disgust, I thought to myself yet again, *God loves that poor, wretched, blinded being who is under the influence of Buddhism.* Yes, that is true, but it is also true that the soul of that poor, misguided, benighted Buddhist fakir was more valuable to Jesus Christ than all the wealth and splendor of this world. Jesus came to earth for this reason—to seek and save the lost—leaving behind the heavenly glory to live a life of pain and agony and shame. It was to seek and to save the lost that He *"became poor, that ye through his poverty might be rich"* (2 Corinthians 8:9). It was to seek and to save the lost that He, *"being in the form of God, thought it not robbery to be equal with God: but made himself of no reputation, and took upon him the form of a servant, and was made in the likeness of men: and being found in fashion as a man, he humbled himself, and became obedient unto death, even the death of the cross"* (Philippians 2:6–8).

Do we have such a love for souls that would be willing to give up the highest earthly honor to take the lowliest place—the place of misunderstanding and rejection and shame and spitting and suffering and death—so that we might save the lost by leading them to know our Lord and Savior Jesus Christ?

His Sensitivity to Opportunities for Saving Souls

In the second place, we see the love of Jesus Christ for souls in His search for favorable opportunities to save perishing souls. We see a striking example in the story of Jesus and the Samaritan woman at the well, which we discussed in the previous chapter. Jesus forgot His own hunger and weariness after a long day's journey in His excitement to share the *"living water"* with this sinner. (See John 4:10–11.)

Another illustration is in John chapter 9 when Jesus went to find the blind man whom the Jews had cast out of the synagogue. Upon finding him, Jesus asked him, *"Dost thou believe on the Son of God?"* (John 9:35). After the blind man asked Him who the Son of God was, Jesus revealed His identity to the man. The man believed in Christ and was healed.

We see still another illustration in Mark chapter 2 where the four friends brought their paralyzed friend to Jesus for healing. The home that Jesus was speaking at was so crowded that the men could not reach Him. Therefore, they went up on the roof, broke through the tiles, and lowered their paralyzed friend down right before Jesus. Jesus saw not only a paralyzed body that needed to be healed but also a lost soul that needed to be saved. Thus, before telling the man to arise, take up his bed, and walk, He told him that his sins had been forgiven. Stalker tells us in his book

Imago Christi that Jesus Christ "made use of His miracles as stepping-stones to reach the soul." We also ought to use every act of kindness that God gives us an opportunity to perform for others as a way to reach souls for Him. We should always be on the lookout for opportunities to save the lost.

Sometime ago, there was a man by the name of Rufus Smith—a quaint man of God—who went up and down the eastern part of England with a passion for saving the lost. I first met him when he was an old man. It was my privilege once to travel with him from Washington to Atlanta. At every station, he would step out of the train and talk to the men on the platform. After his trip, he came to visit me in Minneapolis. He had pneumonia at the time but still insisted on coming to the mission and speaking. After the mission meeting concluded, someone spoke to him about the illumination of the principal business street in Minneapolis. It was only a few blocks away, and he insisted on going to see it. He would not let any expostulation or protest stop him from seeing it. After all, he was well wrapped in a heavy overcoat.

When we reached Nicollet Avenue, there was a blaze of light from the electric arches and he saw a great crowd surging down the sidewalk and filling the roadway. He grew very excited. He turned to me and said, "I can't stand this; I must preach." He tore off his overcoat and handed it to me. After stepping out into the middle of the street, he lifted his voice and said, "Friends, I never saw anything like this, for I am from Missouri. We never have anything like this down there. This is wonderful." The crowd stopped and gathered around him; they thought he was some greenhorn from the country who was stirring up some excitement. His voice rang out again, "I never saw anything like this. This is wonderful." He stopped a moment and then said with intense earnestness, "But this is nothing to what soon shall be. *They that be wise shall shine as the brightness of the firmament; and they that turn many to righteousness as the stars for ever and ever'* (Daniel 12:3)." Then he poured out his soul in a gospel message. We must make use of every opportunity to save souls.

His Search for Lost Souls

In the third place, Jesus Christ's love for souls is seen in His search for lost souls. We see this beautifully set forth by our Lord in Luke 15:4: "*What man of you, having an hundred sheep, if he lose one of them, doth not leave the ninety and nine in the wilderness, and go after that which is lost, until he find it?*" This is from one of the three parables in Luke 15 concerning the lost children of God: the parable of the lost sheep, the parable of the lost coin, and the parable of the lost son. The parable of the lost sheep sets forth the love of Christ Jesus, the Good Shepherd, for the lost; the parable of the lost coin sets forth the love of the Holy Spirit for the lost; and the parable of the lost son sets forth the love of God the Father for the lost.

In this chapter, we are concerned only with the parable of the lost sheep and the love of Christ for the lost. This parable tells us that the Son of God goes after a lost sheep "*until he find[s] it.*" There is a wealth of meaning that we cannot fully extrapolate here, but we do see how deep the Son's love was. Jesus Christ went after lost souls. He not only watched for them and welcomed opportunities to minister to them, but He actively sought opportunities. He not only received the lost when they came to Him; He went after them. A true love for souls will always reveal itself in our active search for them. Are you going out to seek the lost? Most of us think we are doing pretty well (indeed, we are doing better than the average professing Christian) when we commune with the lost when they come to us by attending church. But Jesus Christ went after them. Shall we not do the same?

Some years ago, in Chicago, a young woman attending the Moody Church made it her mission to visit every house and tenement in a section of the city called "Little Hell" to lead all the lost ones to Christ. One day, she knocked on a door and heard a hoarse voice say, "Come in." She entered into a very bare room and saw a dying man lying on a bed in an alcove off of the room. He was dying of quick consumption. She stepped to his side and asked, "Are you a Christian?" "No," he savagely replied, "I am an infidel."

She said nothing more about Christianity, giving only a few kind words before she got up to leave. The next day, she took him a pot of jelly; the next, a pot of jam; the next, some other delicacy. She kept this up for a month. Then, one Sunday afternoon, she came to me at the close of my Bible class and said, "Mr. Torrey, there is a man dying down on Townsend Street, and he is an infidel. I do not think he has long to live. I know you are busy and wish to prepare for your evening service, but won't you come and say a few words to him before he dies?" I hurried with her to this wretched tenement. She took me in and, after introducing me, slipped away.

I sat down by the dying man's bed and asked if I could read the Scriptures to him. He said that I might. I read some passages that told of the love of God for the sinner. Then I read him passages that told how the Lord Jesus Christ had died on the cross for our sins and how all our sins had been laid upon Him. Then I read John 3:16, telling not only of the love of God but also how all that anybody had to do who wanted to be saved was to simply believe on the Son of God. Then I asked him if I might pray with him, and he permitted me to do so. I knelt down beside that wretched bed and asked God to open that dying infidel's eyes to see that there was a God and that God loved him. I prayed that he would see that because Jesus Christ, the Son of God, died for him, all he had to do to find forgiveness and be saved was to believe in Christ.

Then I asked God that He would lead this man to faith in Christ before I finished my prayer. Afterward, the man said, "Amen." Then, as best I could, I began to sing, still kneeling by the bed:

> Just as I am, without one plea,
> But that Thy blood was shed for me,
> And that Thou bidd'st me come to Thee,
> O Lamb of God, I come! I come![1]

I sang verse after verse, until I reached the last verse, when the dying man joined in with me. He had evidently heard the hymn sometime in his childhood at church or Sunday school, and it still remained in his mind. He sang with me, word for word,

> Just as I am, Thou wilt receive,
> Wilt welcome, pardon, cleanse, relieve,
> Because Thy promise I believe,
> O Lamb of God, I come! I come![2]

I looked up and said, "Did you really come?" and he replied, "I did." I arose and explained to him more fully the way of life found in the Scriptures. When I left, he was still rejoicing in Christ. He passed away that very night into eternity as a saved man. And he was saved because a humble woman walked in the footsteps of her Master, seeking out and saving the lost.

His Joy and Satisfaction in Saving Souls

In the fourth place, we see the love of Jesus Christ for souls in that He found His joy and satisfaction in saving lost souls. We will look once again at John chapter 4 for a striking illustration of this. After the Samaritan woman left the well, and the disciples offered Jesus the food they had gathered, He said to them, *"I have meat to eat that*

---

1. Charlotte Elliott, "Just as I Am, Without One Plea," 1835.
2. Ibid.

ye know not of" (John 4:32). The disciples asked among themselves if anyone had brought Him something to eat. Jesus said to them, *"My meat is to do the will of him that sent me, and to finish his work"* (verse 34). He had found such joy in reaching this soul that he forgot about His tiredness and weariness. Is this so with you? Is saving souls your very food and drink? Is saving souls your very joy and satisfaction?

On another occasion, He was so tied up in his work that He had no time to *"so much as eat bread"* (Mark 3:20). When His friends heard of it, *"they went out to lay hold on him: for they said, He is beside himself"* (verse 21). Here, we see that Jesus so lost Himself in His work of saving souls that He neglected the ordinary needs of His body, even to the point that His friends thought He was insane. Another striking illustration of this is in Luke chapter 9. Jesus had just heard of the death of John the Baptist, and His heart was burdened with the loss of His dear cousin and friend. The apostles had just returned from a missionary tour and had *"told him all that they had done"* (Luke 9:10). As He took them aside into a secluded place to rest, the multitudes saw Him and followed Him. Instead of avoiding them, Christ *"received them, and spake unto them of the kingdom of God, and healed them that had need of healing"* (Luke 9:11). What was rest to Him? Here was an opportunity to save souls, and, as much as He needed a time of rest, He found greater satisfaction and joy in saving the lost.

His Celebration over Lost Souls Being Found

In the fifth place, the love of Jesus Christ for souls was seen in His celebration over lost souls that were found. This comes out in the parable of the lost sheep, to which we have referred previously. Christ said,

> When he [the shepherd] *hath found it [the lost sheep], he layeth it on his shoulders, rejoicing. And when he cometh*

home, he calleth together his friends and neighbours, saying unto them, Rejoice with me; for I have found my sheep which was lost. I say unto you, that likewise joy shall be in heaven over one sinner that repenteth, more than over ninety and nine just persons, which need no repentance.   (Luke 15:5–7)

As a shepherd rejoices over his lost sheep when he finds it; as the woman rejoices over her lost coin when she finds it; as the gold-hunter rejoices over gold when he finds it; as the merchant-man rejoices over the pearl when he finds it—so our Lord Jesus rejoices over a lost soul that is found. Oh, how cold and uninterested most of us are when we deal with a soul; and if, perchance, we succeed in leading one to accept Christ, how listless and indifferent we are about it. If you found a diamond worth $1,000, you would be so excited and glad that you would probably have trouble sleeping that night. But if you found and won a soul for Christ, it would probably awaken scarcely a ripple of enthusiasm. This is not so with our Lord Jesus. When He found one lost sheep, *"he layeth it on his shoulders, rejoicing. And when he cometh home, he calleth together his friends and neighbours, saying unto them, Rejoice with me; for I have found my sheep which was lost"* (Luke 15:5–6).

His Grief over Defiant Souls

In the sixth place, the love of Jesus Christ for souls is seen in His grief over souls that refused to be saved. We see this in many of our Lord's actions and words. Take, for example, what Jesus says in John 5:40: *"Ye will not come to me, that ye might have life."* In order to understand these words, we must take a look at the context and tone in which they were spoken. The Lord Jesus came into this world, as we have seen, to save men and to give them life. He went all throughout the land offering this life to men as a free gift. He was soon to die a death of agony and disgrace and most awful shame to make this life possible for them. He offered a renewed life to all of those who came freely to Him. The sadness was that many, like it is even today, would not come. They would gather in enormous crowds to see His miracles and be healed of their infirmities and to listen to His words, but to Himself they would not really come. One day when Christ was surrounded by a great crowd of these miracle-seekers and curiosity-mongers, He stretched out His yearning arms toward them and cried, yes, I think He almost sobbed it out, *"Ye will not come to me, that ye might have life"* (John 5:40).

Oh, I wish I could reproduce the look, the tone, the gesture with which he uttered these words; the look of the tenderest compassion, the tone of sorrowing, heartbreaking love, the gesture of infinite yearning. We have another illustration of this same compassion in Matthew 23:37, where Jesus moaned, *"O Jerusalem, Jerusalem, thou that killest the prophets, and stonest them which are sent unto thee, how often would I have gathered thy children together, even as a hen gathereth her chickens under her wings, and ye would not!"* No woman has ever grieved over her stolen jewels, no mother has ever grieved over a lost child like Jesus grieves over lost men who refused to be saved. No words can tell of the agony that shoots through the heart of Jesus Christ when men refuse to come to Him that they might have life. Do we share His sorrow? Do we feel the pain for lost souls? Do we do everything in our power to bring men and women to a decision for Christ? And if they will not come, do our hearts break over them in pity and love or are we peeved and indignant that they will not yield to our skillful persuasion? Oh, if we had a love like this for souls, many would be won. I know some who have such a love and are constantly winning souls.

The story has often been told, but it bears repeating, of the old deacon who had a great burden for an infidel blacksmith in his village. For months, the deacon studied all the infidel arguments and the replies given in books of Christian evidences. Then he called on the blacksmith in his shop and engaged him in conversation, but the blacksmith was still more than a match for the deacon. Every time he tried this, the deacon would be silenced every few minutes. Finally, the deacon broke into tears and said, "All I can say is, I have deep spiritual concern for your soul." The deacon went home and said to his wife, "Wife, I am only a botch on God's work. I have been studying for months all the infidel arguments and answers and thought I had them all mastered. But when I went down to the blacksmith, he whipped me to a standstill in only a few moments. I am only a botch on God's work." Then he went to his room alone, just off the porch, and kneeled down, saying, "Oh God, I am only a botch on Thy work. I have been studying for months to meet the arguments of the blacksmith, but when I went to talk with him, he put me to silence. O God, Thou knowest I have a love for the blacksmith's soul, but I am only a botch on Thy work."

No sooner had the deacon left the blacksmith's shop than the blacksmith began thinking over his words. He went back into his house and said to his wife, "Wife, I thought I knew all the arguments for Christianity, but the deacon used an argument this morning I had never heard before. He said that he had a 'deep spiritual concern' for my soul. What does he mean?" The wife was a canny woman, and she replied, "You better go ask him." The blacksmith hung up his apron and went to the deacon's house. As he came up to the porch, he heard the deacon's voice through the shutter, praying, "O God, Thou knowest I am only a botch on Thy work." The blacksmith pushed the door open and said, "Deacon, you are no botch on God's work. You have used an argument I had never heard before. You said you had a 'deep spiritual concern' for my soul, and I have come over to ask you to pray for me." How wonderful! Oh, if only we had a deep spiritual concern for the souls of lost men and women. Oh, that we had a love like our Lord's for lost souls, so much so that we would grieve over those who would not be saved.

His Gladness in Laying Down His Life

In the seventh place, the love of Jesus Christ for souls is seen in the fact that He gladly laid down His life to save souls. In John 10:11, Jesus Christ said, "*I am the good shepherd: the good shepherd giveth his life for the sheep.*" We see His sacrifice again in Matthew 20:28: "*The Son of man came not to be ministered unto, but to minister, and to give his life a ransom for many.*" Here is the crowning proof of our Lord's consuming passion for the salvation of the lost. He laid down His life to save the lost, and He laid it down gladly. There was but one way in which sinners could be saved, and that was through the atoning sacrifice of the perfect One. "*Without shedding of blood* [there] *is no remission*" (Hebrews 9:22). The incarnate Son of God, the eternal God, was the only Person in the universe who, by His absolutely sinless character, could make that atoning sacrifice. He said, "I will make it; I will pay the price of man's salvation. I will give up My life in sacrifice for him. I will make propitiation by the shedding of My blood."

Even here, we should follow in His steps. "*He that saith he abideth in him ought himself also so to walk, even as he walked*" (1 John 2:6). Not that we can make atonement. There is no need for that. An absolutely perfect and sufficient atonement has already been made. But we do need to lay down our lives to save the lost. Are you willing to lay down your life for perishing men? Are you willing, if need be, to sacrifice your life so that the vile outcast and the thousands who are lost in the blackest heathenism may live and be saved? Are you ready to face the cholera in China, the plague in India, the blackwater fever in Africa, in order to reach and save the thousands who live in the pestilential parts of the earth? Oh, that is what we need today—men and women who are willing to follow Christ, laying down their lives so that others may live eternally. Raising untold millions by the

Interchurch World Movement or any other movement will avail nothing unless men and women have the spirit of Christ; that is, the love for souls like Christ's and the willingness to lay down their lives to save others.

5

HIS COMPASSION

*"But a certain Samaritan, as he journeyed, came where he
was: and when he saw him, he had compassion on him,
and went to him, and bound up his wounds, pouring in oil
and wine, and set him on his own beast, and brought him to
an inn, and took care of him. And on the morrow when he
departed, he took out two pence, and gave them to the host,
and said unto him, Take care of him; and whatsoever
thou spendest more, when I come again, I will repay thee....
Go, and do thou likewise."*
—Luke 10:33–35, 37

*"He that saith he abideth in him ought himself also so to
walk, even as he walked."*
—1 John 2:6

T hus far, we have studied four features of the picture that God
has drawn in His Word of the real Christ—His holiness, His love

for God the Father, His love for men, and His love for souls. Now we will look at a fifth feature in that picture—His compassion. Though I have done a lot of study on this subject in the past, I did not realize just how much material there is in the Bible about it. With that said, this chapter is just as much a benefit to me as it is for my readers. I hope it will open your eyes to what God has to say about compassion in the picture He has drawn of the Christ in the four Gospels.

In opening, I wish to call your attention to the second Scripture listed above. It is, as you probably recognized, taken from the story of the Good Samaritan. Anyone who really understands this story must see in it the picture of Jesus Christ Himself. It is Christ alone who fully answers to the picture He has drawn of Himself here. He tells us in this story what we should do, but He also tells what He Himself has already done.

What I have discovered regarding the compassion of the real Christ will be organized into two sections: the objects of Christ's compassion and the way in which His compassion was manifested.

The Objects of Christ's Compassion

Who were the objects of Christ's compassion?

The Multitude

First, *"the multitude"* was the object of His compassion. Christ's compassion on the multitude is mentioned five times throughout the Gospels. Matthew 9:36 reads, *"But when he saw the multitudes, he was moved with compassion on them, because they* fainted, and were scattered abroad, as sheep having no shepherd." Jesus had compassion on the multitude because they were distressed and scattered as sheep without a shepherd. This is just as true a description of the multitude in our Lord's day as it is today. Oh, how the great mass of men today are scattered and distressed without a shepherd!

Suppose our Lord Jesus was physically in Los Angeles today. How would He feel about the heedless, thoughtless multitudes who congregate in our streets and parks, our places of amusement, our seaside and mountain resorts? How does the Lord feel today as He looks upon the millions of distressed individuals in China and other lands? The attitude of our Lord toward the multitude, the ordinary herd of men, "the masses," as distinguished from the classes, was in striking contrast to the attitude of the other religious leaders of that day, namely, the scribes and Pharisees. They regarded the multitude as "cursed." When Nicodemus lifted his voice in favor of Jesus, the Pharisees said, *"Have any of the rulers or of the Pharisees believed on him? But this people who knoweth not the law are cursed"* (John 7:48–49). Likewise, the attitude of many of our religious leaders today toward the multitude is more like that of the Pharisees than that of Christ. Why would it matter to them what became of "the mob," "the crowd," "the masses," "the common herd," so long as they had the people of intelligence and position and wealth and influence? There is no question how we ought to feel if we are real Christians, if we are followers of the real Christ. How do you feel toward the great mass of heedless men and women—the multitude?

In Mark 8:2, the hunger of *"the multitude"* moved Christ to compassion. He said, *"I have compassion on the multitude, because they have now been with me three days, and have nothing to eat."* It was not only the spiritual destitution of men that appealed to Christ's compassion but also their physical needs.

In Matthew 14:14, it was simply seeing the crowd that moved the Lord to compassion. We read, *"And Jesus went forth, and saw a great multitude, and was moved with compassion toward them, and he healed their sick."* When Jesus saw a crowd of men, He was moved with compassion. A crowd of men is a pitiful sight. It represents so much sorrow, so much need, so much pain, so much sin. What do you feel when you look at a crowd? Is it mere curiosity? Is it contempt? Is it indifference? Or is it compassion? Judging from this passage, Christ also seems to have a special compassion on the sick.

Those Who Had Lost Loved Ones

Second, Jesus Christ had compassion on those who had lost loved ones. We see a beautiful and touching example of this in Luke 7:12–13:

> *Now when he came nigh to the gate of the city, behold, there was a dead man carried out, the only son of his mother, and she was a widow: and much people of the city was with her. And when the Lord saw her, he had compassion on her, and said unto her, Weep not.*

The woman was a perfect stranger to our Lord, but, as He saw her deep and bitter sorrow over the loss of her only son, His whole heart was stirred with compassion. We read in Hebrews 13:8 that He is just the same today: *"Jesus Christ the same yesterday, and to day, and for ever."* (Hebrews 13:8). Ah, how many lonely, sorrowful ones think that no one cares? Jesus cares.

On the other hand, how unlike Christ Jesus are the Christian Scientists. They have no compassion on the bereaved. No, not for a moment. "There is no such thing as death," they say. "Those who you think are dead have only passed on. You must not weep, and I won't weep with you." It is true that Jesus told the woman in Luke 7 not to weep, but that was only because He was about to restore life back to her son again. Furthermore, when Jesus saw Mary and Martha weeping at Lazarus' tomb, Jesus wept, too, even though He knew their sorrow would be only for a moment. Nevertheless, their sorrow was real; and, just as they sorrowed, so did Christ. Oh, what an utter difference there is between the conduct of the unmotherly "Mother Eddy," the false Christ of Christian Science, and the conduct of our Lord Jesus, the real Christ. One of the most loathsome features of Christian Science is its conduct toward the sorrowing ones. It is cold, heartless, brutish, and selfish, lacking any sympathy or compassion.

All Men

Third, Jesus Christ had compassion on all men, regardless of the form of affliction they suffered, regardless of the type of misfortune, misery, wretchedness, or degradation. In Matthew 20:34, we are told that He had compassion on two blind beggars at the gate of Jericho. In Mark 9:22–25, we are told that He had compassion on a poor, demon-possessed boy. In Mark 1:40–41, we are told that He had compassion on a leper. The world in Jesus' day met the leper with repulsion and disgust and scorn. Christ met him with compassion. The world drew away from him; Christ drew toward him. Every form of misfortune and misery touched Christ's heart. He entered into it as if it were His own. Here, again, we see the difference between the real Christ and the "Christ" of Christian Science.

A Christian Scientist has no compassion on the sick. A sick individual only awakens reproach. "You have no right to be sick," says the Christian Scientist. "You are in error." "Sickness is only illusion, mortal thought." But Jesus, the real Christ, had compassion on the sick and healed them without charge. On the other hand, a Christian Scientist practitioner heals an imaginary sickness (a sickness that is only in the mind) with an imaginary healing (a healing that is also only in the mind) for real money (money that is not only in the mind but also in the practitioner's palm and subsequently put into the practitioner's bulging bank account).

Jesus Christ did not go about His work with a cold sense of duty. On the contrary, He had compassion on those whom He helped and saved. His deeds of mercy cost Him more than leisure time and the expenditure of effort and power. They cost Him heartaches. He made other men's sorrows His own sorrows, other men's agony His own agony, other men's sin and shame His own sin and shame. He could not look upon misery, sickness, pain, death, and sin without feeling hurt Himself. We read in John 11:33, "*When Jesus therefore saw her weeping, and the Jews also weeping which came with her, he groaned in the spirit, and was troubled.*" Herein lay the great secret to His power. It is the misery we make our own that we can comfort; it is the wants and needs we make our own that we can fully satisfy; it is the sin we make our own that we can save another from. We read Christ's example of this in Paul's letter to the Corinthians: "*For he hath made him to be sin for us, who knew no sin; that we might be made the righteousness of God in him*" (2 Corinthians 5:21). Real power to help men is a very expensive thing, but we learn that anyone can have it who is willing to pay the price. The one who is not willing to give up his lightness of heart and carry someone else's burden of sin and sorrow and shame might as well give up on trying to help anyone. Men cannot be saved by burning words. No! Only by bleeding hearts.

In Dundee, Scotland, lives a Christian woman of wealth and position. Her interest is not in society and fashion but in the poor, needy, fallen, and outcast. One time, a very depraved and much hardened woman was brought to the Home for the Fallen, in which she was very interested. The woman was dying from the

consequences of her sin and every attempt someone had made
to introduce her to the Lord Jesus had failed. Her time on earth
was growing very short. Now the woman of wealth and position,
the true follower of the real Christ, went to see her. As she tried
to speak to her about the Savior she so sorely needed, the dying
woman grew only more and more angry, hard, and bitter. With a
breaking heart, the Christlike woman leaned over the dying sinner
and could not keep her tears from falling onto her cheek. Instantly,
the dying girl's heart softened, and she listened to the woman. She
saw Jesus and believed in Him! She said afterward, "It was the
tear that did it." Oh, how this sorrow-stricken, sin-ruined world
of ours, staggering toward its doom, needs men and women with
compassion like our Lord's!

The Compassion of Christ Manifested

Now we are going to take a look at some tangible ways in which
Christ's compassion manifested itself. In learning about Christ's
compassion, may we look for ways in which to apply His examples
to our own lives.

In His Willingness to Share Our Sorrows

First, Christ's compassion was manifested in His willingness
to take the sorrows of others as if they were His own. We see this
in John 11:33–36:

> *When Jesus therefore saw her weeping, and the Jews also
> weeping which came with her, he groaned in the spirit, and
> was troubled, and said, Where have ye laid him? They said
> unto him, Lord, come and see. Jesus wept. Then said the Jews,
> Behold how he loved him!*

As we have already seen, the sorrow of these bereaved sisters was only temporary, for Jesus would heal their brother in a matter of moments. Nevertheless, their sorrow was real, and Christ took notice of it, even to the point of joining in it.

Paul instructs us also to *"weep with them that weep"* (Romans 12:15). Oh, how little some of us do this. I have spoken of the utter heartlessness of the Christian Scientists and their principles as an essential part of their religion; but there is altogether too much heartlessness in professedly evangelical Christians, which is diametrically opposed to their religion, to the example of their Lord, and to the teaching of the entire Bible. We are too busy sometimes to enter into the sorrow of others and to *"weep with them that weep."* But the real Christ, in spite of all the work that was crowded into His three-and-a-half years of public life, was not too busy to stop to *"weep with them that weep."* We read in Matthew 20:30–34 that when Jesus was hurrying toward the most urgent business of His life—His death on the cross—two blind beggars in misery called out to Him. The disciples rebuked them and told them not to bother the great Master with their petty sorrows when He was on such an important mission. However, we read that *"Jesus stood still, and called them"* (Matthew 20:32). Oh, that we were more like Him, never too busy to sympathize with the suffering, no matter how insignificant they appear to be in the eyes of the world.

In His Selfless Ministrations to the Needs of Others

Second, the compassion of Jesus Christ was manifested in His selfless, persistent, and thorough ministrations to the needs of others. This is graphically set forth in the story of the Good Samaritan in Luke chapter 10. As I have already said, the Good Samaritan is a picture of the Lord Jesus Christ Himself. Note that when the Samaritan saw the poor, wounded, robbed, stripped, naked, dying man, *"he had compassion on him"* (Luke 10:33). But that is not all. His compassion was not of that shallow, unreal sort that evaporates shortly after a moment of sentiment, tears, and expressions of sympathy. Rather, he *"went to him, and bound up his wounds, pouring in oil and wine, and set him on his own beast, and brought him to an inn, and took care of him. And on the morrow when he departed, he took out two pence, and gave them to the host, and said unto him, Take care of him; and whatsoever thou spendest more, when I come again, I will repay thee"* (Luke 10:34–35). His compassion was characterized by action—self-sacrificing action. He put the wounded man *"on his own beast."* He walked so that the sufferer might ride; he went without so that the sufferer might have. He took the sufferer to an inn, stayed with him, paid his bill, and provided for his future need. His action was persistent and thorough. It did not last a mere hour but until the weak man could fend for himself. Ah, such was the compassion of Christ, and such should be ours. *"He that saith he abideth in him ought himself also so to walk, even as he walked"* (1 John 2:6).

In His Patience

Third, the compassion of Jesus Christ was manifested in His patience in teaching His followers, healing the sick, and feeding the hungry. In Mark 6:34, we read, *"And Jesus, when he came out, saw much people, and was moved with compassion toward them, because they were as sheep not having a shepherd: and he began to teach them many things."* Christ, at this time, was very weary at heart. He had just heard of the death of His cousin and faithful friend, John the Baptist, and had gone aside with His disciples for a time of quiet rest. But when He saw the crowd, the great unshepherded mob of common people, His heart was moved with compassion. He forgot His own weariness and sorrow as He looked into the eyes of those neglected people. He decided to spend the whole day with them, teaching them the great truths of the kingdom using simple illustrations, so that they could understand. Indeed, they *"heard him gladly"* (Mark 12:37).

He taught them before He fed them, for the need of their souls was far deeper and far greater than the needs of their bodies. So it is today that the intellectual and spiritual needs of the masses are far greater than their physical needs, great as those are. Likewise, one who has a wise, Christlike compassion will minister to others' spiritual and moral needs before their physical needs. It is often said that Jesus fed the bodies of men before He sought to teach and save them, but the inspired record tells us differently. Our Lord was not so foolish as to try to reach the superficial need before tending to the deeper spiritual need that underlay it. Here is where the "social service" enthusiasts are making a colossal blunder at home and in the foreign field. We would do well to follow in our Master's steps.

However, Jesus did not stop with ministering to the spiritual needs of people. He also ministered to their physical bodies—their hunger and their sickness. He fed and healed them. In Matthew's account of the event we have been discussing, we read that *"Jesus went forth, and saw a great multitude, and was moved with compassion toward them, and he healed their sick"* (Matthew 14:14). In Matthew 15:32, we read, *"Then Jesus called his disciples unto him, and said, I have compassion on the multitude, because they continue with me now three days, and have nothing to eat: and I will not send them away fasting, lest they faint in the way."*

Christianity exalts the spirit of man, but it does not forget or neglect the body. It first teaches and heals the spirit, and then it feeds and heals the body. "Social service" is all right if we put it in its right place. Our Lord's compassion began with the spiritual needs of the multitude, but it did not end with them. The salvation that the real Christ brings is salvation for *"spirit and soul and body"* (1 Thessalonians 5:23). Notice that the spirit comes first.

The manifestation of Christ's compassion in teaching the unshepherded is one we can imitate, even if we have no money to feed the hungry or the gift of healing to help the sick. If you can do nothing else, you can teach some lost child on the street.

In His Healing Ministry

Fourth, the compassion of Jesus Christ was manifested in His healing ministry. We see an example of this in Mark 1:40–41: *"And there came a leper to him, beseeching him, and kneeling down to him, and saying unto him, If thou wilt, thou canst make me clean. And Jesus, moved with compassion, put forth his hand, and touched him."* When one stops to reflect on this incident and our Lord's action in it, there is something exquisitely beautiful about it. For years, that leper had not felt the touch of a clean and loving hand. His nearest friends and dearest relatives had abandoned him. He was indeed an outcast. Whenever a clean man approached him, he was forced to betray his misfortune and warn others not to touch him by crying out in a strained, hoarse, uncanny voice, "Unclean, unclean."

In this example, the man approaches Jesus and cries, *"If thou wilt, thou canst make me clean."* The heart of our Lord goes out to him in infinite compassion, and as He stretches forth His hand and touches him, the man is healed. There are many moral lepers today who need and long for the touch of a clean hand—a touch that will heal them. Ah, but we shrink away. How the holy woman shrinks away from the vile woman on the street; how the holy man shrinks away from the lecherous man, the moral leper. This is natural and right, up to a certain point. However, if one wishes to help and save, his compassion must triumph over moral aversion and get near enough to the sinner to reach out his hand and touch him. You cannot save sinners at the end of a forty-foot pole. You must get into touching distance; you must touch them for Christ.

When Mr. Alexander and I were in Bolton, England, we made a midnight sweep of the streets and gathered the drunkards who poured out of the pubs into a procession to the armory. Three or four thousand men and women, many of whom were drunk, were brought into the building. It was an awful-looking company of men and women. Mrs. Alexander decided to sit with a degraded, bloated, loathsome-looking woman she'd found on the streets during the meeting and dealt with her afterward. This repulsive-looking woman turned to Mrs. Alexander and said, "You do not love me." Mrs. Alexander replied, "Yes, I do." "Kiss me, then," she cried. So Mrs. Alexander kissed her and won her for Christ.

On one of my last visits to Chicago, a man came to me whom I had known years before. The first time we had met was when John Woolley had sent him to me after his professed conversion. He had been a drunkard and a crook, and he soon returned to his old lifestyle. Many men tried to rescue him but every attempt failed. He simply worked the people who tried to help him. After a few years of this had passed, I had the opportunity to meet up with him. He came to me as I stepped down from the platform and said to me,

> Mr. Torrey, I am a saved man now. I have been saved for some time and have been helping save others. But now I am going fast with consumption, and I wanted to see you before I die. That is the reason for my visit tonight. I have a good position. I need nothing, but I wanted to tell you something. I have never forgotten the day you knelt beside me and put your arm around me and talked to me and prayed for me. I have fallen time and time again since but have still often felt your arm about me. Even in the prison cell, I have felt your arm around me, and, Mr. Torrey, that is what led me at last to really accept Christ and be saved. I

am dying and have not many months to live, but I felt that I must tell you this before I died.

Oh, friends, this world is full of men like that, full of women like the one Mrs. Alexander kissed, and they are just longing for real compassion—the compassion that gets right alongside of them and touches them and saves them. The man of whom I have been speaking was one of the most unlikely men to be helped by such an act of kindness. Never did I feel more like telling a man to be gone than I did to him. I knew he was a crook. I knew he was a professional worker of kindhearted people, and that they are among the most hopeless of men, but compassion conquered and saved even him.

In His Welcome and Pardon of Sinners

What we have said leads naturally into the fifth way in which the compassion of Jesus Christ manifested itself. It was manifested in Christ's welcome and pardon of the sinner. One of the greatest examples of this is found in a passage we looked at earlier in our discussion of the love of the real Christ for men. It is found in Luke chapter 7. A woman who was a notorious outcast in Capernaum had heard Jesus say, "*Come unto me, all ye that labour and are heavy laden, and I will give you rest*" (Matthew 11:28). This message had reached her heart and led her to believe in Him. When the crowd dissolved, she spotted Jesus entering the house of Simon, a Pharisee. After returning home to retrieve her costly alabaster box of expensive ointment, she hurried back to Simon's house, walked through the open door, approached Jesus as He reclined at the table, and poured her ointment on His bare feet, wetting them with her tears and wiping them with her hair.

Simon and the other guests were shocked that the Lord allowed such a woman, so notorious a sinner, to touch Him. The

Lord had compassion on the woman, vile and sunken as she was, and looked into her teary eyes. *"Thy sins are forgiven,"* He said; *"Thy faith hath saved thee; go in peace"* (Luke 7:48, 50). We, too, must welcome the sinner and bid him go in peace instead of turning away in disgust.

Here are two thoughts to ponder before we close this chapter on our Lord's compassion. First, Jesus Christ, the real Christ—the only real Christ—is just the same today as He was when He walked on this earth: *"Jesus Christ the same yesterday, and to day, and for ever"* (Hebrews 13:8). Second, *"He that saith he abideth in him ought himself also so to walk, even as he walked"* (1 John 2:6). It is sometimes difficult to follow our Lord Jesus, the Christ of God, in His holiness, and even far more difficult to follow in His compassion. We do not live in a compassionate age. We may talk as we please about the "brotherhood of man," and we may multiply our humane societies and our Red Cross societies, but our almsgiving, our social services, and our general helpfulness are often of an institutional character, lacking a warm, personal element. They lack the touch of Christlike compassion. We act through various social agencies instead of going forth as our Lord Jesus did and stepping into the lives of the sorrowful, the distressed, and the diseased. We must actually live alongside of them, pouring out our love and compassion to broken people. Even we preachers want to save men from the pulpit rather than touching them in their need, sorrow, and sin. Church members are very alike in this way. Oh, brethren, quit it. Follow in the steps of the real Christ and get out among men, among the poor, the sorrowing, the sick, the sinful. Make their sorrows your own, like Christ did. Then and only then can you save them.

6

HIS MEEKNESS

*"Take my yoke upon you, and learn of me; for I am meek
and lowly in heart: and ye shall find rest unto your souls.
For my yoke is easy, and my burden is light."*
—Matthew 11:29–30

*"Now I Paul myself beseech you by the meekness
and gentleness of Christ."*
—2 Corinthians 10:1

*"Tell ye the daughter of Sion, Behold,
thy King cometh unto thee, meek, and sitting upon an ass,
and a colt the foal of an ass."*
—Matthew 21:5

Thus far, we have studied five features of the real Christ, the
Christ of actual fact, as distinguished from the "Christ" of man's

fancies and dreams. We have studied the picture of Christ God has drawn in His Word. We have studied His holiness, His love for God the Father, His love for men, His love for souls, and His compassion. Now we will take a look at a sixth feature in that picture, a feature that is in close connection with the last we studied, His compassion, but which, at the same time, is quite distinct from it. Our subject in this chapter is the meekness of Jesus Christ.

The three texts listed above emphasize the fact that the Lord Jesus was meek. In the second text, His lowliness and meekness are closely connected. At first, I thought of combining these two into one feature, but I found that the material was too abundant; therefore, though they are closely related, they are entirely separate and distinct features in the portrait. The meekness of Christ is one thing; the lowliness and humility of Christ is quite another.

What Is Meekness?

The first question that confronts us is, What is meekness? We shall find it is something quite different from the ordinary idea of meekness. The thought that the word *meekness* conveys to the average mind, that indeed it formerly conveyed to my own mind, is that of "patient submissiveness under injustice and in jury." Now, Jesus exhibits this submissiveness, as we shall see in the future when we study His humility; but that is not what the Bible means by "meekness." The Greek word that is translated into "*meek*" in our texts means, according to its usage in Greek literature from the time of Homer until now, "gentle" or "mild." The word in its Bible usage means the same. I have looked up the sixteen passages in the Bible in which the word and its derivatives are found, and I have discovered that the connections in which the word is used clearly show that the meaning of "meekness" is the attitude of mind that is opposed to harshness and contentiousness, the attitude of mind that shows itself in mildness and gentleness and tenderness in its dealings with others. The predominant idea of meekness, then, is having gentleness in dealing with others and correcting their errors.

The other texts listed above are perfect examples of this gentleness. Jesus says in Matthew 11:29, *"Take my yoke upon you, and learn of me; for I am meek and lowly in heart: and ye shall find rest unto your souls."* The thought here is that we will find rest in being led by Jesus, because He is a gentle teacher and master. This is made even clearer in the following verse: *"For my yoke is easy, and my burden is light"* (Matthew 11:30). The Greek word that is translated here as "easy" really means "mild," "kind," "pleasant," or "gracious." We see in 2 Corinthians 10:1 that Paul couples the word *"meekness"* with *"gentleness,"* thus alluding to their close connection: *"Now I Paul myself beseech you by the meekness and gentleness of Christ."* That gentleness is also distinguished from the warlike spirit mentioned in Matthew 21:5: *"Tell ye the daughter of Sion, Behold, thy King cometh unto thee, meek, and sitting upon an ass, and a colt the foal of an ass."* Here, Jesus' meekness is associated with His sitting on an ass, the beast of burden and service, as distinguished from sitting on a horse, an animal associated with war throughout the Bible.

The Manifestation of Christ's Weakness

That the thought of gentleness and mildness and tenderness in dealing with others and correcting their errors is the thought of God in speaking of the meekness of Christ will become more evident as we consider the second question, How was the meekness of Christ manifested?

In His Gentle Dealings
with the Spiritually Lukewarm

In the first place, the meekness of the Christ was manifested in His gentle dealings with those whose spiritual life was fragile, the flame of whose love to God was flickering. This comes out beautifully in Isaiah's prophetic vision of the coming Christ as quoted in Matthew 12:20: *"A bruised reed shall he not break, and smoking flax shall he not quench."* (See Isaiah 42:1–3.) The feeble, flickering faith and love of many is here compared to the reed that is bruised and almost broken and the wick that is smoking and almost extinguished. The Lord Jesus will treat all, not with the severity and sternness that will crush and extinguish, but with the tenderness that will strengthen and fan into a flame.

It is a lesson we can all learn in dealing with those who are young in the Christian life and weak in their faith. There is a great danger in discouraging these by expecting too much of them and demanding too much from them. Many who were once a reed that was nearly broken are today a stalwart oak, able to resist any violent storm, and many who were once like a smoldering wick about to go out are now a brightly shining light for God. But many well-meaning yet tactless and unchristian zealots for the truth crush many bruised reeds and quench many smoking wicks. Oh, that we were all more like our Lord in this. He dealt in the most considerate, delicate, and exquisitely tender way with the broken. With a gentle breath, He flamed the spark into a fire instead of quenching it with a much too vigorous gust.

In His Gentle Dealings with Sinners

Second, the meekness of the Christ was manifested in His gentleness in dealing with sinners. He rebuked penitent sinners, forgave them, and bid them go in peace. We see this illustrated in the incident we have already referred to in Luke 7. Simon and the other guests would have driven the sinful woman from the house in righteous indignation if she had tried to wash their feet. However, when she approached Jesus, He looked into her teary eyes and saw the dawning of a better life and the budding faith inside of her. He said to her, *"Thy sins are forgiven....Thy faith hath saved thee, go in peace"* (Luke 7:48, 50). Which are we more like, our Lord Jesus or Simon the Pharisee?

Many years ago, in my first pastorate in an outstation, a woman who had been a notorious sinner came to me and asked to be water baptized. We gathered a pool of water, and I submerged her, along with her past, beneath the baptismal water. Then she was raised again into newness of life. Still, some good people—really good people, I think—thought it was dreadful that I should baptize a woman like that so soon after her conversion. Though they were good people in many ways, this concern of theirs was certainly unlike the Lord. Some of the saintliest people I have ever met were once the vilest of the vile. Fortunately for them, in the beginning of their Christian life, they had been touched by someone who had learned of the meekness of Christ.

I know a man who is loved and honored by thousands—loved and honored as few are loved and honored on both sides of the Atlantic—but was one of the wickedest and vilest of men until he was converted at forty-two years of age. He was converted, very thoroughly converted, but was still extremely sensitive, weak, and easily discouraged. He came to Chicago as a young convert and became acquainted with people who loved him and trusted him, in spite of the black record of his past. But he had grave discouragements still. One day, he was sorely discouraged and was invited to a friend's house—one who had welcomed him to his hearth, yes, to the very heart of his own home circle. A little child who could scarcely talk ran eagerly to him. He took her up in his harms arms, and she, throwing her arms around his neck, whispered, "I love oo,

Coby." It was a message of hope and cheer from heaven, spoken through infant lips. It saved him to Christian service, a service in which he has been marvelously blessed. Suppose he had been received with severity, with cold words and suspicion, and excluded from that family circle—where would he have been today?

In His Tender Words to Those Who Wronged Him

Third, the meekness of the real Christ was manifested in His tender words to those who had wronged Him. In Mark, we read a story about a woman who had an issue of blood and who tried to receive Christ's blessing by touching His garment. It was unseen by many men, but Christ turned to her and said, *"Daughter, thy faith hath made thee whole; go in peace, and be whole of thy plague"* (Mark 5:34). This woman had been ill for many years with a disease that kept her from associating with the clean. *"When she had heard of Jesus, [she] came in the press behind, and touched his garment. For she said, If I may touch but his clothes, I shall be whole"* (Mark 5:27–28).

She was a coward. She should have openly confessed what He had done before the confession was wrung from her, but the Lord Jesus did not spurn her on that account. He gently asked who had touched His garment. It seemed like a foolish question to the disciples, for many were crowding around Him and, in that sense, touching Him, but only one had really "touched" Him. The trembling woman was full of fear. She knew she had done wrong. She was afraid He would drive her away and that she would lose the blessing. But, with indescribable gentleness, He turned to her and said, *"Daughter, thy faith hath made thee whole; go in peace, and be whole of thy plague"* (Mark 5:34).

This woman richly deserved reproof. She deserved to go without the blessing she sought from trying to obtain it in an underhanded way, without rendering to the Lord Jesus the acknowledgment and honor He so richly deserved. But the gentleness and tenderness of our Lord! He did bring out the public confession of her former need and present healing, but in an ever so gentle way. Our Lord could have been severe; He could have been scathing in His rebukes. Ah, yes, but He was more mild and gentle than the gentlest mother. That is an art we all need to learn more fully and practice more regularly. You might say, "That is not my natural temperament." Then, get a supernatural temperament. Get it by yielding to the supernatural grace that transforms a wrong temperament into a Christlike temperament; get it by the filling of the Holy Spirit, for *"the fruit of the Spirit is love, joy, peace, longsuffering, gentleness, goodness, faith, meekness, temperance: against such there is no law"* (Galatians 5:22–23).

In His Gentleness with Doubters

Fourth, the meekness of Christ was manifested in the gentleness He had with doubters. This we see in the case of Thomas. You might recall the story, as recorded in John 20:24–28, of how Thomas was not present with the other disciples when our Lord appeared to them. And you might recall, too, that when Thomas returned to the apostolic company, the disciples cried in unison, *"We have seen the Lord,"* and then Thomas undermined their declaration, saying, *"Except I shall see in his hands the print of the nails, and put my finger into the print of the nails, and thrust my hand into his side, I will not believe"* (John 20:25). A week passed and Thomas remained in his unbelief. The next week, when Jesus came and revealed Himself to Thomas, He said to him, ever so gently (I often wonder what His face looked like at the time), *"Reach hither thy finger, and behold my hands; and reach hither thy hand, and thrust it into my side: and be not faithless, but believing"* (John 20:27).

Just like Thomas, there are many doubters today, many stubborn, willful doubters, who can be won by this kind of treatment. But we try to pound our beliefs into their heads. We get angry and contentious and argumentative and self-assertive when they do not accept our beliefs at once. We will never win them with this attitude. We simply confirm their doubt and unbelief. You say that they are unreasonable. Yes, they are unreasonable, and you are un-Christlike. Thomas was most unreasonable. He was stubborn and willful, saying that unless he was given the exact kind of proof he demanded, he would not believe, no matter how sufficient other proofs might have been. As unreasonable as Thomas was not to believe the competent testimony of the men whom he knew so well, and as willful as he was in trying to dictate just what kind of proofs he must be given to believe, our Lord Jesus was still gentle and kind. Soon, we see Thomas on his knees, looking up into the face of Jesus and crying, *"My Lord and my God"* (John 20:28).

I saw a man like that last summer in China. I watched him with keen interest. He was gentle and courteous with everyone—the Chinese as well as the Europeans, the Chinese coolie as well as the Chinese gentleman, the stubborn skeptic as well as the enthusiastic believer in Christ—and he won them all. I saw little children flock around him and drink in every word he had to say. I saw prominent scholars defer to him. I saw a proud Chinese gentleman yield to him and, with alacrity, do what he himself was very loath to do. Where had he learned it? He had learned it from the Lord Jesus, to whom he had turned in early childhood. Many of us were converted later in life and were harsh, overbearing, self-assertive, and dominating before we were converted. As a result, we have brought much of our severity and dominating self-assertion into our witness for Christ, trying to bend everyone toward our point of view. Instead, may we learn from Christ's example today.

In His Tender Rebukes

Fifth, the meekness of Christ was manifested in the tenderness with which He rebuked self-confidence, unfaithfulness, and betrayal. One of the best examples we have of this is Peter's denial, which we read about in Matthew chapter 26. You might remember what Peter said on the night before the crucifixion: *"Though all men shall be offended because of thee, yet will I never be offended"* (Matthew 26:33), and again, *"Though I should die with thee, yet will I not deny thee"* (verse 35). You might remember, too, how, a little later, when faced with a charge made by a servant girl, *"Are not thou also one of this man's disciples?"* (John 18:17), Peter's courage instantly vanished, and his protestations of loyalty were utterly forgotten. He denied the Lord three times, the last denial coupled with oaths and curses.

Now, Jesus is risen from the dead, and Peter meets Him on the shores of Galilee. After breakfast, the Lord inquires of Peter, *"Simon, son of Jonas, lovest thou me more than these?"* (John 21:15), and Peter answers, *"Yea, Lord; thou knowest that I love thee"* (verse 15). Then Jesus adds, *"Feed my lambs"* (verse 15). This happens again a second time, and then a third time; but on the third time, the Lord says, as He looks into Peter's teary eyes, *"Simon, son of Jonas, lovest thou me?"* (John 21:17). With tearing streaming down his cheeks, Peter answers, *"Lord, thou knowest all things; thou knowest that I love thee"* (verse 17). Again, Jesus says, *"Feed my sheep"* (verse 17).

Oh, how wonderfully tender Christ was! Searching, it is true, but how tender! How gentle! And all the more effective because He was gentle. Peter was grieved all the more deeply because Christ was so gentle. Peter never forgot this incident, and he never denied his Lord again. When standing before the very council that had condemned Christ to death, he said,

Ye rulers of the people, and elders of Israel, if we this day be examined of the good deed done to the impotent man, by what means he is made whole; be it known unto you all, and to all the people of Israel, that by the name of Jesus Christ of Nazareth, whom ye crucified, whom God raised from the dead, even by him doth this man stand here before you whole. This is the stone which was set at nought of you builders, which is become the head of the corner. Neither is there salvation in any other: for there is none other name under heaven given among men, whereby we must be saved.   (Acts 4:8–12)

Peter was filled with even more love for Christ because of His gentleness toward him.

Now we should the time to ask ourselves how differently some of us would have treated Peter. We would have received him back; oh, yes, but what a sound trouncing we would have first given him. I can imagine myself handling Peter and saying fiercely in righteous indignation, "Simon, you coward, you poltroon, denying your Lord with oaths and curses. You ought to be ashamed of yourself. You ought to go and hide your head. You ought to hesitate to show yourself in the presence of His disciples." Ah, how unlike we are to Him whom we call Lord.

In His Tender Reproof of His Betrayers

Sixth, the meekness of the Christ was manifested in His tender and pleading reproof of His betrayers. We see Christ's response to Judas Iscariot's betrayal in John chapter 13. *"Jesus...was troubled in spirit, and testified, and said, Verily, verily, I say unto you, that one of you shall betray me"* (John 13:21). Later, when He had given the sop to Judas, and he took it, Satan thus entering him, Jesus turned to him and said, *"That thou doest, do quickly"* (John 13:27). What tenderness, what pleading there was in His response. Try to imagine the tone in which Jesus said it. It is true that the Lord's meekness failed to bring Judas to repentance, but the devil had already entered Judas, and the devil, alas, is incorrigible, even before the meekness and gentleness of our Lord.

The same thing happened in the garden of Gethsemane, when Judas came with the priests and soldiers to arrest Jesus and drag Him to trial and crucifixion. Judas brazenly approached Jesus and kissed Him again and again in seeming affection. Despite his outward affection, his kisses were only to mark Him as the one to arrest. Our Lord said, with eyes full of pity and a voice full of compassion, *"Judas, betrayest thou the Son of man with a kiss?"* (Luke 22:48). Our Lord would have won Judas if it were possible. If anything could have succeeded, that would have.

In His Prayers for His Murderers

Seventh, the meekness of Christ manifested itself in His prayers for His murderers—the very ones who nailed Him to the cross. I hardly need repeat the story to many of you. Jesus is hanging on the cross. He is in awful agony—physical agony, yes, but far more mental and spiritual agony; for the whole weight of man's sins has been laid upon Him *"who knew no sin"* (2 Corinthians 5:21). Therefore, He recoils in horror from sin like no other man has ever recoiled, for no other has ever been as holy as He. The Father's face is hidden from Christ by the black cloud of our sin. His heart is breaking, and He soon cries, in an agony such as no other son of man ever knew, *"My God, my God, why hast thou forsaken me?"* (Matthew 27:46).

Now, from the cross, He looks down on those who, only moments before, drove the nails into His hands and feet and left Him hanging on the cross. As He sees them gambling for the garments they have stripped from His poor body, He utters a

prayer—not a prayer of execration but a prayer of wondrous pity—
"Father, forgive them; for they know not what they do" (Luke 23:34).

I cannot go on. The sublime simplicity and pathos of the divine record make impossible all attempts at human exposition. I do not need to attempt it. Go meditate upon it alone and never forget that *"he that saith he abideth in him ought himself also so to walk, even as he walked"* (1 John 2:6).

7

HIS HUMILITY

"Take my yoke upon you, and learn of me; for I am meek and lowly in heart: and ye shall find rest unto your souls for my yoke is easy, and my burden is light."
—Matthew 11:29–30

"Now before the feast of the passover, when Jesus knew that his hour was come that he should depart out of this world unto the Father, having loved his own which were in the world, he loved them unto the end. And supper being ended, the devil having now put into the heart of Judas Iscariot, Simon's son, to betray him; Jesus knowing that the Father had given all things into his hands, and that he was come from God, and went to God; he riseth from supper, and laid aside his garments; and took a towel, and girded himself. After that he poureth water into a basin, and began to wash the disciples' feet, and to wipe them with the towel wherewith he was girded....Ye call me Master and Lord: and ye say well; for so I am. If I then, your Lord and Master,

have washed your feet; ye also ought to wash one another's
feet. For I have given you an example, that ye should do as I
have done to you."
—John 13:1–5, 13–15

"He that saith he abideth in him ought himself also so to
walk, even as he walked."
—1 John 2:6

Thus far in our study of the picture of the real Christ, which God has given us in His own Word, we have looked carefully at six features: His holiness, His love for God the Father, His love for men, His love for souls, His compassion, and His meekness. Now we look at another feature that is very intimately connected with His meekness—that is, His humility.

Our subject is the humility of the real Christ, not the Christ men dream about and paint from their own fancies upon canvas or write about in their own words, but the Christ who actually existed, who actually lived on this earth among men, and who left an example for us so that we might *"walk, even as he walked"* (1 John 2:6). The whole secret of a really successful life here on earth is to walk in His steps. The more closely we follow His steps, the more successful our lives will be.

In the first of these texts, we learn that Jesus of Nazareth, who was crucified by the rulers of His people, was the real Christ of God. In the first text, Christ states the fact that He was lowly and humble of heart. In the second text is an amazing illustration of His humility and His response that anyone who desires to be accounted as one of His disciples must follow Him in this. In the third text is an emphatic teaching—anyone who claims to abide in Him must make good his claim by walking as He walked.

Humility is a distinct Christian virtue. It was regarded with contempt by the world's ethical philosophers until the Lord Jesus came and exemplified it in His own life and then demanded it of all His followers. Xenophon, Plato, and Isocrates all used the Greek word translated *"lowly"* in Matthew 11:29 with contempt. They often used it to signify pusillanimity, or cowardice, as did Isocrates. Epictetus, in some respects one of the greatest Greek ethical philosophers, uses a word derived from the Greek term for "lowly" to signify pusillanimity, as does the Jewish historian and moralist Josephus. The Bible alone reveals that humility is a virtue found only in the teaching and example of Christ Jesus, the real Christ.

What Is Humility?

The first question that we will look at here is, What is humility? It is a tremendously important question, for much that is dubbed "humility" is, in reality, pusillanimity or hypocrisy, as in the classical example of Uriah Heep, the protagonist of Charles Dickens's novel *David Cooperfield*. Just what real humility is, we shall see by considering how the humility of the real Christ manifested itself.

How the Humility of Christ Manifested Itself

In His Refusal to Seek His Own Glory

First, the humility of the Christ of God is manifested in His refusal to seek His own glory. This we see in John 8:50, where

Christ says, "*I seek not mine own glory.*" Christ's own glory meant nothing to Him, but the Father's glory was everything. It mattered nothing to Him what He might suffer in body or mind or reputation; if God were glorified by it, He chose it. He put a right comparative estimate on His own glory and on that of the Father. "*My Father is greater than I*" (John 14:28) was not a solitary utterance of Christ Jesus; it was the keynote of all His thinking and living.

If we are to be like Him, we, too, must put our own glory behind us, completely out of sight. It must be of no avail to us. God's glory must not only be supreme but everything we live for. It must our only motive for action in all departments of our lives. There is a right, of which we are not possessors, that Jesus had for making His own glory at least a secondary consideration after that of the Father: He possessed all of the divine attributes in all their fullness. In Him dwelt "*all the fulness of the Godhead bodily*" (Colossians 2:9). But even He, while equal with the Father in nature and attributes, never lost sight of His subordination to the Father and made His own glory absolutely nothing. Do we follow His lead in this?

In His Avoidance of Praise

Second, the humility of the real Christ was manifested in His avoidance of praise. We see this first in the following prophetic statement and afterward in Christ's actual life here on earth. Isaiah put it this way: "*He shall not cry, nor lift up, nor cause his voice to be heard in the street*" (Isaiah 42:2). Praise was not something Jesus sought; it was something He shunned. He tried as much as possible, when His compassion compelled Him, to perform miracles of healing, to perform them in obscurity, bidding those who were healed to tell no one. How unlike Him many of us are in this respect. He shunned praise; we court it. He sought to prevent the advertisement of Himself; we have, or wish we had, an advertising bureau. Ah, it is fine to dream and write songs about being Christlike. It would not be as fine, to some of us, at least, to really be so.

In Association with Outcasts

Third, the humility of Jesus Christ was manifested in His intimate association with the despised and outcast. We are told in Matthew 9:10 that *"it came to pass, as Jesus sat at meat in the house, behold, many publicans and sinners came and sat down with him and his disciples."* Our Lord was not like the social and religious snobs of that day. It was a cause of frequent complaint on the part of the religious aristocracy of the day—the Pharisees and scribes— that Jesus *"receiveth sinners, and eateth with them"* (Luke 15:2). Our Lord did not consider Himself too good, too cultured, or too blue-blooded (though He was of royal lineage) to associate in intimate and friendly fellowship with the most despised people. It was good, red blood that coursed through His veins, rather than "blue" blood, or poisoned venous blood.

Alas, in some churches today, many consider themselves quite above intimate fellowship with other church members. I attended a church service in an eastern city some years ago. The church that morning was receiving members from one of their missions—poor people. I had a friend in the congregation, a woman of wealth and culture and social prominence, who was a member of the church. I noticed that she did not rise when these members from the mission were welcomed into the church. I said to her afterward, "Why did you not stand when the members from the mission were received into the church?" "Oh," she replied, "I could not say what the covenant says regarding them. I have no intention of associating with them." And yet she was a woman with a benevolent spirit far beyond many others. She even used her money largely for the elevation of the poor. However, it was not at all so with our Lord.

No one was too poor or too sinful for His companionship and fellowship. He knew that He was the Son of God—the King of Kings and Lord of Lords—but He had no sense of superiority over the poorest and most despised. In fact, there was nothing of that nauseating, patronizing air of condescension in His association with the poor and sinful that affects so many today, who fancy that they have a superior culture, social position, or morality. Of all snobs, the pious snob is the most offensive.

In His Submission to Injury and Injustice

Fourth, the humility of Jesus Christ was manifested in His willing and joyful submission to outrageous injury and injustice. Isaiah prophesied this kind of submission on Christ's part in Isaiah 50:5–6: "*The Lord God hath opened mine ear, and I was not rebellious, neither turned away back. I gave my back to the smiters, and my cheeks to them that plucked off the hair: I hid not my face from shame and spitting.*" This prophecy of the humility of the Christ, which was fulfilled seven hundred years later, was about the real Christ who lived here on earth. He literally gave His back to the smiters and His cheeks to those who that plucked out His hair. He hid not His face from shame and spitting. He submitted willingly, yes, even joyfully, to outrageous injury and injustice from men, that He might glorify God by saving the very ones who thus maltreated Him. How nearly like Him are we in this? How nearly like Him in this do we care to be?

In His Reaction to Ridicule

In the fifth place (and here we go a step further), the humility of Jesus Christ was manifested in His reaction to ridicule and abuse. We see that Christ remained silent during persecution in Isaiah 53:7: "*He was oppressed, and he was afflicted, yet he opened not his mouth: he is brought as a lamb to the slaughter, and as a sheep before her shearers is dumb, so he openeth not his mouth."* Ah, it is easy to bear grave injustice and outrageous injury if we can talk back and voice our injured innocence, our exalted sense of martyrdom. But to suffer and say nothing, not even to call the attention of others to what a pure and noble martyr you are—that is humility, the genuine article, the humility of the real Christ, Jesus.

In His Silence Against False Accusation

Sixth, we see the humility of Jesus Christ in that He did not stand up for Himself under false accusation. We see this time and time again in the Word of God. For example, 1 Peter 2:23 says, "[Jesus], *when he was reviled, reviled not again; when he suffered, he threatened not; but committed himself to him that judgeth righteously.*" And in Matthew 26:59–63, we read,

> *Now the chief priests, and elders, and all the council, sought false witness against Jesus, to put him to death; but found none: yea, though many false witnesses came, yet found they none. At the last came two false witnesses, and said, This fellow said, I am able to destroy the temple of God, and to build it in three days. And the high priest arose, and said unto him, Answerest thou nothing? What is it which these witness against thee? But Jesus held his peace, and the high priest answered and said unto him, I adjure thee by the living God, that thou tell us whether thou be the Christ, the Son of God.*

Luke tells us in Luke 23:8–10,

> *And when Herod saw Jesus, he was exceeding glad: for he was desirous to see him of a long season, because he had heard many things of him; and he hoped to have seen some miracle done by him. Then he questioned with him in many words;*

but he answered him nothing. And the chief priests and scribes stood and vehemently accused him.

Our Lord Jesus did not defend His good name. He left that to God; He *"committed himself to him that judgeth righteously."* This is a lesson that we, in this day, sorely need to learn. Many have learned it at least in part, but how often we forget. So, I emphasize it today, lest we forget.

In His Reason for Coming to Earth

Seventh, the humility of Jesus Christ was manifested in one of the reasons He came to this earth: to minister, not to be ministered to. One of the most deeply significant and suggestive utterances that came from Christ's lips is found in Matthew 20:28: *"The Son of man came not to be ministered unto, but to minister, and to give mis life a ransom for many."* Ah, that is humility—to really consider yourself the servant of all and, consequently, to seek to serve all and be served by none. That is not natural, I suppose, to any of us. We wish to be waited upon rather than to wait upon others; and if, for the time being, we must serve, we are ever looking forward to the time when we shall be served, and are constantly building castles in the air, in which there are hosts of servants, and we ourselves are the grandees who are being served. Even in the church, we covet the office where others dance to tend to us instead of the lowly place of service in which we must do the bidding of others. The word *minister* originally meant "servant," but nowadays it too often means the "boss of the whole show." We are greatly concerned about the prerogatives and dignity and respect due to the minister. And the word *deacon* also originally meant "servant," but now it means various degrees of dignity. Oh, let us remember the words of the Master, *"The Son of man came not to be ministered unto, but to minister, and to give his life a ransom for many."*

In His Service to Others

Eighth, the humility of Jesus Christ was manifested in His humble, menial, and, at times, repulsive service for others. He came to serve; even more than that, He served in the lowliest forms of service. This we see in one of our texts, John 13:1–5:

> Now before the feast of the passover, when Jesus knew that his hour was come that he should depart out of this world unto the Father, having loved his own which were in the world, he loved them unto the end. And supper being ended, the devil having now put into the heart of Judas Iscariot, Simon's son, to betray him; Jesus knowing that the Father had given all things into his hands, and that he was come from God, and went to God; he riseth from supper, and laid aside his garments; and took a towel, and girded himself. After that he poureth water into a basin, and began to wash the disciples' feet, and to wipe them with the towel wherewith he was girded.

It was a slave's work that Jesus performed here. He and His disciples had come in from the dusty road and, in the Eastern custom, laid aside their sandals; but there was no servant to perform the customary and necessary feet washing for them, and none of the disciples would do it for the others. Each felt it was beneath his dignity. And so our Lord, in full consciousness of His divine authority and origin, "*knowing that the Father had given all things into his hands, and that he was come from God*," arose, laid aside His garments, girded Himself with a towel, took the basin, and went from disciple to disciple, washing their dirty feet.

I wonder why the painters who have given us their various representations of so many scenes in the life of Christ never painted that scene. In this connection, our Lord specifically emphasized the fact that He had given us an example that we should follow. How closely are you imitating the example that Jesus left? Would you rather be a minister by preaching sermons to a crowd of gaping admirers or a minister by washing the sore and foul feet of some afflicted child of God? "Oh," but you say, "my social position and official dignity will not permit me to stoop to service of that character." Remember what we are told about Jesus in this very connection, that it was with the full knowledge of His divine authority—*"The Father had given all things into his hands"*—and with the full knowledge also of His divine origin and mission and destiny—*"He was come from God, and went to God"*—that He did all these things.

At one time, I knew a young woman in Christian work in Chicago. For some reason, I did not have a very high estimate of the depth of her piety. She belonged to a very well-known family, and I imagined that she was altogether too conscious of it. But, one day, someone came and told me how she had gone into one of the poorest parts of Chicago, into "Little Hell," and, finding a poor, afflicted creature in bed with sore and vile feet, she had unbound those feet with her own hands and cheerfully, pleasantly, and thoroughly washed them. From that day on, I could not but have a higher estimation of the real Christlikeness of that young woman.

In His Decision to Dwell in the Lowliest Place

Ninth, the humility of the Christ of God was manifested in His choice to dwell in the lowliest place of contempt as a slave instead of the loftiest place of glory as God. This choice antedated His entry into human history as an integral part of it all. It began in the eternal glory. We read about it in that marvelous statement of Paul that we have had occasion to quote so often: "[Jesus Christ] *being in the form of God, thought it not robbery to be equal with God: but made himself of no reputation, and took upon him the form of a servant, and was made in the likeness of men"* (Philippians 2:6–7). Oh, what sublime humility there was in stooping from the glory of occupying the throne of the universe—the center and object of angelic, cherubic, and seraphic worship—to take the form of a servant. It is in this connection that Paul exclaims with tremendous emphasis, *"Let this mind be in you, which was also in Christ Jesus"* (Philippians 2:5).

Yes, this is the mind of the real Christ, the "mind of the Master." It is not primarily some doctrinal statement of faith, no matter how rigidly and completely orthodox it seems; it is the mind of surrender. He surrendered the very highest position and took the very lowest, forsaking the place of highest honor and seeking for Himself the lowliest and, therefore, the most effective, service. It was because He revealed His true humility by seeking the lowest place any man ever occupied that our Father said,

> *Wherefore God also hath highly exalted him, and given him a name which is above every name: that at the name of Jesus every knee should bow, of things in heaven, and things in earth, and things under the earth; and that every tongue should confess that Jesus Christ is Lord, to the glory of God the Father.*
> (Philippians 2:9–11)

In His Obedience to the Father

Tenth, the humility of Jesus Christ was manifested in His being obedient to the Father, whatever the cost. We see this in the verse we were just talking about. Christ, *"being found in fashion as a man...humbled himself, and became obedient unto death, even the death of the cross"* (Philippians 2:8). Here, we reach the highest point of Christ's lowest humility, not merely God becoming man—the highest of all lords becoming the lowest of all servants—but becoming the Sin-Bearer of the vilest of sinners. No other one whom human eyes have ever seen has occupied, by natural, divine, and eternal right, so high a position of dignity, honor, glory, and worship as He. And no other ever stooped as low as a death of agony and shame, accursed of God and man. Again, it is because of this that the Spirit of God says, through Paul, *"Let this mind be in you, which was also in Christ Jesus"* (Philippians 2:5). John also had this in mind when he wrote, *"He that saith he abideth in him ought himself also so to walk, even as he walked"* (1 John 2:6).

8

HIS MANLINESS

*"And it came to pass, when the time was come that he should
be received up, he stedfastly set his face to go to Jerusalem."*
—Luke 9:51

*"He that saith he abideth in him ought himself also so to
walk, even as he walked."*
—1 John 2:6

Thus far, we have studied seven features of the picture God has
drawn of the real Christ in His Word: His holiness, His love for
God the Father, His love for men, His love for souls, His compassion, His meekness, and His humility. The last three here—His
compassion, His meekness, and His humility—are very closely
associated. Now we are going to take a look at another characteristic of our Lord that is of a very different sort—His manliness. In
most of the paintings of our Lord, His face is not only, to a marked

degree, womanly; it is marked positively effeminate and weak. The same is true of the pictures of Christ Jesus drawn in the words of many preachers. It is not a true picture of the real Christ. They dishonor the Lord. Gentle He was, as we have already seen, and gentleness is more frequently a characteristic of women than of men—of mothers, wives, and daughters than of fathers, husbands, and sons.

How Christ's Manliness Manifested Itself

While He was more gentle than the gentlest mother—the gentlest Person who ever lived on this earth, the one true and perfect *Gentleman*—He was at the same time the strongest and most virile of all the sons of men. Gentleness and humility and meekness are seldom found coupled with energy and virility. I do not think that the term "manliness" altogether accurately conveys what I mean, for many women display many of the qualities I am about to describe more fully than most men. What we men, in our presumption and arrogance and self-sufficiency, call "manliness" is just as much, if not more, in actual life, "womanliness." But I use the term "manliness" because it comes nearer to describing to the average mind what I mean than any other term of which I can think.

I recall reading a book more than forty years ago called *The Manliness of Jesus.* I have entirely forgotten the contents of that book. Nevertheless, the book made a deep impression upon me at the time, and I presume that it suggested the title of this chapter. Just what I mean by "manliness" will become clear as we come to consider how the manliness of the real Christ (not the "Christ" whom artists paint from their own fancies, but the Christ who actually lived on this earth and whose perfect portrait God Himself has drawn in the Bible) was manifested.

In His Fearlessness in the Face of Peril

First, as we see in these texts, the manliness of Christ was manifested in His absolute fearlessness in the face of gravest peril. This comes out again and again in the story of His life here on earth. Look, for example, at Luke 9:51: *"And it came to pass, when the time was come that he should be received up, he stedfastly set his face to go to Jerusalem."* Our Lord Jesus knew He was going to Jerusalem to face shame, suffering, agony, and death. Like mentioned before, no other has ever naturally shrunk from death as He did because no other has been as full of life as He was. But He looked in the eye the fast-approaching suffering and agony and shame—yea, death himself—without flinching. He marched to meet him, to feel his sting, and to conquer him. We see the same thing from a different angle in John 18:3–8:

> *Judas then, having received a band of men and officers from the chief priests and Pharisees, cometh thither with lanterns and torches and weapons. Jesus therefore, knowing all things that should come upon him, went forth, and said unto them, Whom seek ye? They answered him, Jesus of Nazareth. Jesus saith unto them, I am he. And Judas also, which betrayed him, stood with them. As soon then as he had said unto them, I am he, they went backward, and fell to the ground. Then asked he them again, Whom seek ye? And they said, Jesus of Nazareth. Jesus answered, I have told you that I am he: if therefore ye seek me, let these go their way.*

The underlying significance of these words, spoken under such circumstances, is obvious. We see much the same thing in John 12:27–28: "*Now is my soul troubled; and what shall I say? Father, save me from this hour: but for this cause came I unto this hour. Father, glorify thy name. Then came there a voice from heaven, saying, I have both glorified it, and will glorify it again.*" The shadow of the cross lay athwart the pathway Jesus trod from the beginning of His public ministry. This is evident from the words He uttered on His first visit to Jerusalem after the beginning of His public ministry. "*Jesus answered and said unto them, Destroy this temple, and in three days I will raise it up*" (John 2:19). Knowing that He would have to endure unutterable horrors—horrors inconceivable to our finite minds—from the outset the cross, He still marched right toward it without swerving from the path God had marked out, undeceived and unbeguiled by the popularity that His beneficent ministry had awakened at first.

We must follow this manly fearlessness. We must follow Him in the face of the gravest peril, for He has said in Matthew 16:24, "*If any man will come after me, let him deny himself, and take up his cross, and follow me.*"

In the Boldness of His Utterances

In the second place, the manliness of the Christ of God was manifested in the boldness of His utterances. We see this in His words before the high priest Annas and the Roman governor, Pilate, as John recalls:

> *The high priest then asked Jesus of his disciples, and of his doctrine. Jesus answered him, I spake openly to the world; I ever taught in the synagogue, and in the temple, whither the Jews always resort; and in secret have I said nothing. Why askest thou me? Ask them which heard me, what I have said*

unto them: behold, they know what I said. And when he had thus spoken, one of the officers which stood by struck Jesus with the palm of his hand, saying, Answerest thou the high priest so? Jesus answered him, If I have spoken evil, bear witness of the evil: but if well, why smitest thou me?... Then Pilate entered into the judgment hall again, and called Jesus, and said unto him, Art thou the King of the Jews? Jesus answered him, Sayest thou this thing of thyself, or did others tell it thee of me? Pilate answered, Am I a Jew? Thine own nation and the chief priests have delivered thee unto me: what hast thou done? Jesus answered, My kingdom is not of this world: if my kingdom were of this world, then would my servants fight, that I should not be delivered to the Jews: but now is my kingdom not from hence. Pilate therefore said unto him, Art thou a king then? Jesus answered, Thou sayest that I am a king. To this end was I born, and for this cause came I into the world, that I should bear witness unto the truth. Every one that is of the truth heareth my voice.

(John 18:19–23, 33–37)

The story continues in chapter 19:

When Pilate therefore heard that saying, he was the more afraid; and went again into the judgment hall, and saith unto Jesus, Whence art thou? But Jesus gave him no answer. Then saith Pilate unto him, Speakest thou not unto me? Knowest thou not that I have power to crucify thee, and have power to release thee? Jesus answered, Thou couldest have no power at all against me, except it were given thee from above: therefore he that delivered me unto thee hath the greater sin.

(John 19:8–11)

Even bolder are Christ's words before the high priest Caiaphas.

*And they that had laid hold on Jesus led him away to Caiaphas
the high priest, where the scribes and the elders were assembled....Now the chief priests, and elders, and all the council,
sought false witness against Jesus, to put him to death; but
found none: yea, though many false witnesses came, yet found
they none. At the last came two false witnesses, and said, This
fellow said, I am able to destroy the temple of God, and to
build it in three days. And the high priest arose, and said unto
him, Answerest thou nothing? what is it which these witness
against thee? But Jesus held his peace. And the high priest
answered and said unto him, I adjure thee by the living God,
that thou tell us whether thou be the Christ, the Son of God.
Jesus saith unto him, Thou hast said: nevertheless I say unto
you, Hereafter shall ye see the Son of man sitting on the right
hand of power, and coming in the clouds of heaven.*

(Matthew 26:57, 59–64)

In His Warrior Spirit

In the third place, the manliness of the Lord Jesus was manifested in His warrior spirit. The Lord Jesus came *"to heal the
brokenhearted"* (Luke 4:18), to comfort the sorrowful and the
heavy laden (see Matthew 11:28), to gently bind up all the gaping
wounds of humanity. But He also came to be the dauntless leader
in the fiercest fight the universe has ever known. We see this
again and again in Scripture. Matthew 10:34 will probably serve
to illustrate this as well as any passage in God's record: *"Think not
that I am come to send peace on earth: I came not to send peace, but
a sword."*

Jesus Christ was indeed the Prince of Peace, but He was also
the Prince of Warriors. The hymn "The Son of God Goes Forth to
War" has great truth in it. So does the following hymn by Samuel
Stennett:

Majestic sweetness sits enthroned
Upon the Savior's brow;
His head with radiant glories crowned,
His lips with grace o'erflow,
His lips with grace o'erflow.[3]

The peace the real Christ preached was peace through victorious warfare. To be a true follower of Jesus, the Christ of God, one must be a fearless fighter as well as a gentle comforter.

Today, the fight is hotter than ever before in this old world's history; for the end draweth nigh, and Satan rages, for he knows his time is short. Today, we sorely need warrior Christians. If we are to preach a full gospel, we must preach a gospel of hard, fierce, but completely victorious, warfare.

In His Frank Dealings with Men

In the fourth place, the manliness of Christ Jesus was manifested in His utter and fearless frankness in dealing with men. It is illustrated in Luke 9:57–58: "*And it came to pass, that, as they went in the way, a certain man said unto him, Lord, I will follow thee whithersoever thou goest. And Jesus said unto him, Foxes have holes, and birds of the air have nests; but the Son of man hath not where to lay his head.*" We see it again in Luke chapter 14:

And there went great multitudes with him: and he turned, and said unto them, If any man come to me, and hate not his father, and mother, and wife, and children, and brethren, and sisters, yea, and his own life also, he cannot be my disciple. And whosoever doth not bear his cross, and come after me, cannot be my disciple. For which of you, intending to build a tower, sitteth not down first, and counteth the cost, whether he have sufficient to finish it? Lest haply, after he hath laid

3. Samuel Stennett, "Majestic Sweetness Sits Enthroned," 1787.

the foundation, and is not able to finish it, all that behold it begin to mock him, saying, This man began to build, and was not able to finish. Or what king, going to make war against another king, sitteth not down first, and consulteth whether he be able with ten thousand to meet him that cometh against him with twenty thousand? Or else, while the other is yet a great way off, he sendeth an ambassage, and desireth conditions of peace. So likewise, whosoever he be of you that forsaketh not all that he hath, he cannot be my disciple.

(Luke 14:25–33)

Our Lord concealed nothing. He would have all with whom He dealt know the very worst as well as the very best. While He longed to disciple people because He knew that discipleship of Himself meant infinite and eternal blessing for everyone who became His disciple, He would not have one person become His disciple without a full understanding of the tremendous cost of discipleship, without a clear and full apprehension of all the shame and suffering and loss that accompanied it. This is a lesson we modern evangelists and preachers sorely need to learn. We are constantly ringing the changes upon what one gains by coming to and accepting Christ. Our Lord Jesus rang the changes on what one lost by coming to Him. He appealed to the heroism and self-sacrifice of men, as well as their longing for peace and joy and infinite reward.

There is great need today for us to preach a heroic gospel, a gospel of self-sacrifice, and not a gospel that seeks to minimize the sacrifice involved with servanthood. May we not seek to transform the church that Christ Jesus founded, the crucified Christ founded, into a competitor with the dance hall, the card club, the vaudeville, and the movie theater. When the New England Methodist Conference voted to rescind the historic Methodist position regarding questionable amusements—in order that they might allure the weak-kneed manikins and womanettes, who desire be called "Christian" but, at the same time, lead a soft, luxurious, self-indulgent life—they sounded the death knell of real, forceful, Christlike Christianity in that section of Methodism. And if the Quadrennial Conference of the Methodist Episcopal Church follows their example, as many hope they may, they will sound the death knell of the once great and glorious Methodist Church in America.

In His Uncompromising Attitude Toward Sin

In the fifth place, the manliness of Jesus Christ was manifested in His uncompromising attitude toward all sin. This is seen, for example, in His terse but meaningful utterance recorded in John 8:34, *"Jesus answered them, Verily, verily, I say unto you, Whosoever committeth sin is the servant of sin."* Sin was always sin in the eyes of Christ Jesus. There was no such thing as excusable sin or venial sin or little sin, in His estimation. Sin was always, whatever it might be, the same hateful, abominable, ruinous, enslaving thing, for *"whosoever committeth sin is the servant of sin."*

He had compassion upon sinners of all sorts; He hated and denounced sin in all its forms. There was none of that namby-pamby, milk-and-water, half admiring, half palliating attitude toward some forms of sin that is so common, even among certain classes of professed Christians today. Jesus Christ never called a carnival of lust a "romance," as our newspapers do almost every day. No, these were His blistering words: *"Whosoever putteth away his wife, and marrieth another, committeth adultery: and whosoever marrieth her that is put away from her husband committeth adultery"* (Luke 16:18). Sin was sin—hideous, loathsome, enslaving. He cried, *"I tell you, Nay: but, except ye repent, ye shall all likewise perish"* (Luke 13:3). He pardoned sin when it was repented of, but He also sternly added, *"Sin no more, lest a worse thing come unto thee"* (John 5:14). His attitude toward sin was unyielding, strong, virile, and uncompromising. This is a lesson that we need to learn. Sometimes, because of our fondness for the sinner, because he is dear to us by ties of relationship or for some other reason, and because we are trying to emulate Christ's compassion, we are tempted to condone other people's sins. That is utterly un-Christlike. He never did so.

In His Firmness

In the sixth place, the manliness of Christ Jesus is seen in His unbending firmness. This we see, for example, in Luke 9:59–62:

> *And he said unto another, Follow me. But he said, Lord, suffer me first to go and bury my father. Jesus said unto him, Let the dead bury their dead: but go thou and preach the kingdom of God. And another also said, Lord, I will follow thee; but let me first go bid them farewell, which are at home at my house. And Jesus said unto him, No man, having put his hand to the plow, and looking back, is fit for the kingdom of God.*

The requests of these two men, at first glance, seem reasonable. But they are not reasonable to Jesus. He had made a demand upon these men for immediate action. Their call was not only important but imperative. He gently, but nonetheless firmly, said, *"Let the dead bury their dead,"* and then, *"No man, having put his hand to the plow, and looking back, is fit for the kingdom of God."* His response was positive and firm. There was nothing of the weak, vacillating, palavering, sentimental ethical culturist and moral liberalist about Him. He was a man—a full-grown man, God's pattern man.

In His Severe Denunciation of Sin

In the seventh place, the manliness of Christ Jesus was manifested in the severity with which He denounced hypocrisy, unreality, pretence, self-righteousness, self-sufficiency, self-deception, and unconfessed sin. We see this severity in Luke 16:14–15:

> And the Pharisees also, who were covetous, heard all these things: and they derided him. And he said unto them, Ye are they which justify yourselves before men; but God knoweth your hearts: for that which is highly esteemed among men is abomination in the sight of God.

How severe and searching these words of our Lord were, especially when we remember to whom they were spoken—the men who prided themselves not only upon the thoroughness and rigidity of their orthodoxy but also upon the strictness of their morality and the loftiness of their ideals of holy living. But consider again Jesus' words to the scribes and Pharisees:

> But woe unto you, scribes and Pharisees, hypocrites! for ye shut up the kingdom of heaven against men: for ye neither go in yourselves, neither suffer ye them that are entering to go in. Woe unto you, scribes and Pharisees, hypocrites! for ye devour widows' houses, and for a pretence make long prayer: therefore ye shall receive the greater damnation. Woe unto you, scribes and Pharisees, hypocrites! for ye compass sea and land to make one proselyte, and when he is made, ye make him twofold more the child of hell than yourselves. Woe unto you, ye blind guides, which say, Whosoever shall swear by the temple, it is nothing; but whosoever shall swear by the gold of the temple, he is a debtor! Ye fools and blind: for whether is greater, the gold, or the temple that sanctifieth the gold?
>
> (Matthew 23:13–17)

Still further down in the chapter, we read,

> Woe unto you, scribes and Pharisees, hypocrites! for ye pay tithe of mint and anise and cummin, and have omitted the

weightier matters of the law, judgment, mercy, and faith: these ought ye to have done, and not to leave the other undone. Ye blind guides, which strain at a gnat, and swallow a camel. Woe unto you, scribes and Pharisees, hypocrites! for ye make clean the outside of the cup and of the platter, but within they are full of extortion and excess. Thou blind Pharisee, cleanse first that which is within the cup and platter, that the outside of them may be clean also. Woe unto you, scribes and Pharisees, hypocrites! for ye are like unto whited sepulchres, which indeed appear beautiful outward, but are within full of dead men's bones, and of all uncleanness. Even so ye also outwardly appear righteous unto men, but within ye are full of hypocrisy and iniquity....Ye serpents, ye generation of vipers, how can ye escape the damnation of hell?

(Matthew 23:23–28, 33)

Is this the same Christ Jesus we saw earlier, when we studied His compassion and His meekness? Yes, this is the very same Jesus—the real Christ—who was as strong and manly as He was meek and humble in heart. Remember, meekness is not weakness, and humility is not servility. It is true that the religion of Jesus Christ is preeminently a woman's religion: it has lifted woman to an eminence never dreamed of before. But it also just as much a man's religion! Its appeal is for heroism, fearlessness, holy audacity, and self-sacrifice.

In His Acceptance of Agony

Eighth, the manliness of our Lord Jesus was manifested in His glad and unhesitating acceptance of torture and agony. He did not yield one iota of the truth as He faced death on the cross. He died in order to save others from ruin. Our Lord Jesus could have escaped the cross if He had been willing to compromise a little with the religious rulers of the day. Yes, He could have escaped easily, but He did not. He pursued the path of absolute allegiance to God and His truth, though the cross loomed ahead. He did not diverge one step in order to get around the cross. Christ could have escaped when the emissaries of Annas and Caiaphas and the others came to arrest Him in the garden. If He would have but besought the Father, the Father would have instantly sent twelve legions of angels to deliver Him. (See Matthew 26:53.) But He knew that if He escaped the cross, sinners would perish eternally.

On the Mount of Transfiguration, when He was in the process of glorification, He refused the glory there awaiting Him and talked with Moses and Elijah of the death He was about to accomplish in Jerusalem. (See Luke 9:31.) He also turned His back on the glory when He became incarnate (see Philippians 2:6–8), as well as when He went to Jerusalem to die so that you and I might live. You and I must tread the same path if we choose to abide in Him, for it is written in God's Word, *"He that saith he abideth in him ought himself also so to walk, even as he walked"* (1 John 2:6). The path of manly, literal sacrifice of self to save others is the path He trod. He Himself has said, *"If any man will come after me, let him deny himself, and take up his cross, and follow me"* (Matthew 16:24).

9

HIS PEACE, JOYFULNESS, AND OPTIMISM

"I will greatly rejoice in the LORD, *my soul shall be joyful in my God; for he hath clothed me with the garments of salvation, he hath covered me with the robe of righteousness, as a bridegroom decketh himself with ornaments, and as a bride adorneth herself with her jewels."*
—Isaiah 61:10

"These things have I spoken unto you, that my joy might remain in you, and that your joy might be full."
—John 15:11

"Peace I leave with you, my peace I give unto you: not as the world giveth, give I unto you. Let not your heart be troubled, neither let it be afraid."
—John 14:27

Thus far, we have considered eight features in the picture which God has given us in His Word of Christ, and we have seen how each feature adds to the stunning masterpiece of our Savior and

114

Lord. Now we will look at three additional features of Christ that are so closely related, it is almost impossible to altogether separate them. They are, in some respects, closely related to His manliness. In this chapter, we will look at the real Christ—His imperturbable peace, His constant joyfulness, and His unconquerable optimism.

His Imperturbable Peace

We shall first consider the imperturbable peace of the real Christ, the Christ of God's own appointment, Christ Jesus. The whole life of our Lord was characterized by a calm composure—self-possession, divine serenity, and abiding and abounding peace that could not be disturbed. He was always sure of Himself and of the happy outcome of whatever events occurred, no matter how disturbing they appeared to be.

He Had Calm Confidence in the Face of Peril

First, the imperturbable peace of Christ was manifested in His perfect calmness and confidence in an hour of great peril. This we see in Mark 4:37–40:

> And there arose a great storm of wind, and the waves beat into the ship, so that it was now full. And he was in the hinder part of the ship, asleep on a pillow: and they awake him, and say unto him, Master, carest thou not that we perish? And he arose, and rebuked the wind, and said unto the sea, Peace, be still. And the wind ceased, and there was a great calm. And he said unto them, Why are ye so fearful? how is it that ye have no faith?

From parallel accounts in Matthew and Luke (see Matthew 8:23–26; Luke 8:22–25), we see that His disciples were almost beside themselves with fear. Our Lord Jesus Himself was not only perfectly calm and fearless; He was surprised at the disciples' fearfulness, and He gently rebuked it, exclaiming, "*Why are ye so fearful? how is it that ye have no faith?*" The "great calm" that lay upon the sea was nothing compared to the great calm that possessed His own heart.

He Was Confident in the Face of Calamity

Second, the imperturbable peace of Christ Jesus was manifested in the confidence He maintained when facing calamity and bearing the burdens of those whom He dearly loved. We see this illustrated in the story of Jairus and the death of his daughter.

> *While he yet spake, there came from the ruler of the synagogue's house certain which said, Thy daughter is dead: why troublest thou the Master any further? As soon as Jesus heard the word that was spoken, he saith unto the ruler of the synagogue, Be not afraid, only believe. And he suffered no man to follow him, save Peter, and James, and John the brother of James. And he cometh to the house of the ruler of the synagogue, and seeth the tumult, and them that wept and wailed greatly. And when he was come in, he saith unto them, Why make ye this ado, and weep? the damsel is not dead, but sleepeth. And they laughed him to scorn. But when he had put them all out, he taketh the father and the mother of the damsel, and them that were with him, and entereth in where the damsel was lying. And he took the damsel by the hand, and said unto her, Talitha cumi; which is, being interpreted, Damsel, I say unto thee, arise. And straightway the damsel arose, and walked; for she was of the age of twelve years. And they were astonished with a great astonishment. .*
>
> (Mark 5:35–42)

Notice the excitement, the tumult, and the excessive grief of everyone except Christ. He stayed in perfect peace and confidence.

He Had Serenity in the Face of Death

Third, the imperturbable peace of the Christ of God was manifested in His serene and exultant peace when contemplating His death—a death of unparalleled and inconceivable sorrow, shame, and agony. Though His soul was *"exceeding sorrowful, even unto death"* (Matthew 26:38), and His heart was breaking with the weight of man's reproach (see Psalm 69:20), He had a deep, harmonious undertone of perfect peace. This we see, for example, in John 14:1, when He said to His disciples, *"Let not your heart be troubled: ye believe in God, believe also in me."* Gently He said to them, *"Peace I leave with you; my peace I give unto you: not as the world giveth, give I unto you. Let not your heart be troubled, neither let it be fearful"* (John 14:27).

He Displayed Perfect Rest While Bearing Our Sin

Fourth, the imperturbable peace of the Lord Jesus was manifested in His perfect rest as He bore our sin. Jesus remained peaceful even on the cross, when His Father hid His face from Him. Still, He cried out with a heart breaking in unutterable mental and spiritual agony, *"My God, my God, why hast thou forsaken me?"* (Matthew 27:46). Then there came, welling up from the deeper depths of His innermost spirit, that other cry of perfect trust and peace: *"Father, into thy hands I commend my spirit"* (Luke 23:46). As He uttered that last cry of perfect peace and hope and handed His spirit over to the Father, His earthly life ended in a glorious burst of peace that triumphed over death.

We find in this peace what a privilege it is to follow Him. How comforting to know that whatever perils, whatever losses, whatever agonies we may be called upon to face on this earth, they cannot possibly match the sorrow and agony and shame He bore for us. Yet He held on to His peace, even in the face of death.

His Constant Joyfulness

Now let us look at another feature God has portrayed in His picture of the real Christ, His crucified Son—His constant joyfulness.

Isaiah tells us that the coming Christ of God was to be *"a man of sorrows, and acquainted with grief"* (Isaiah 53:3), and he goes on to give us a very detailed and vivid description of the appalling sorrows and grief that would accompany the Messiah. But, immediately after telling us this, he says, *"He shall see of the travail of his soul, and shall be satisfied"* (Isaiah 53:11). In John 16:20–22, Christ's death, and the glory that follows His resurrection, are compared to a woman who has given birth to a child and then looks him in the eye. Our Lord uses the same example when talking to His disciples about the joy that would follow His resurrection after they had suffered through His crucifixion.

It does not stop here. On the night before His crucifixion, with the cross and all its pain fully in view, Christ said to His disciples, *"These things have I spoken unto you, that my joy might remain in you, and that your joy might be full"* (John 15:11). In substance, then, our Lord said, "When My joy—the joy that now fills and thrills My heart—shall be yours, your joy shall be full." The phrase "be full" is translated in the American Standard Version as "made full" and in the Revised Version as "fulfilled." Turn that word "fulfilled" around, and you will get just what Jesus actually said: "Filled full." When you get the same joy that our Lord Jesus had, even when contemplating His own crucifixion, your joy will be "filled full." His joy was fullness of joy—joy filled to the brim. Though He was the Man of Sorrows, our Sin-Bearer, He was, at the same time, the gladdest man who ever walked this earth.

The Sources of His Joy

Obedience to His Father and the Fruit That Followed

The first source of His joy was obeying His Father and bearing fruit for Him. And this is a joy that He wants to share with us: *"These things have I spoken unto you, that my joy might remain in you, and that your joy might be full"* (John 15:11). It is important to notice the verse immediately preceding this: *"If ye keep my commandments, ye shall abide in my love; even as I have kept my Father's commandments, and abide in his love"* (John 15:10). From these words, it is evident that His joy was in doing the Father's will and that He encourages us to do the same.

We see the same thought in John 4:34: *"My meat is to do the will of him that sent me, and to finish his work."* He went on to say, *"Herein is my Father glorified, that ye bear much fruit; so shall ye be my disciples"* (John 15:8). His joy was the joy of bearing fruit for God. Further, these two joys (or this single twofold joy), the joy of obedience to God and the joy of bearing fruit for God, are two of the greatest joys possible to men, as well.

Saving Souls

The second source of the joy of Christ Jesus is connected to the first. It was the joy of saving souls. Again, in a prophetic vision of the coming Christ, Isaiah said, *"He shall see of the travail of His soul, and shall be satisfied"* (Isaiah 53:11). The fruit of the travail of His soul—of the pangs of spiritual parturition—was the multitude of souls that would be saved through His sufferings unto death. Our Lord felt more than compensated for all the agonies He endured. He exultantly cried to the assembled hosts of heaven, *"Rejoice with me; for I have found my sheep which was lost"* (Luke 15:6). Ah, there are few greater joys than the joy of seeing others saved. And this joy can be ours, too! It can be ours if we are willing to pay the price—soul travail.

Completing the Father's Will

The third source of Christ's joy was found in contemplating the Father's will. We see this in Luke 10:21: *"In that hour Jesus rejoiced in spirit, and said, I thank thee, O Father, Lord of heaven and earth, that thou hast hid these things from the wise and prudent, and hast revealed them unto babes: even so, Father; for so it seemed good in thy sight."* The word translated as *"rejoiced"* in this passage is a peculiarly expressive word. It means "to exult" or "to rejoice exceedingly." It is translated as *"exceeding glad[ness]"* in Matthew 5:12 and *"exalted joy unspeakable"* in 1 Peter 1:8. It may seem, at first glance, that this joy is the same as what we talked about in the first point, of Christ obeying the Father, but they are quite different. That was the joy of *doing* the Father's will; this is the joy of *contemplating* the Father's will, in all its wisdom and infinite excellence. This joy, too, can and should be ours.

God Himself

The fourth source of Christ's joy was God Himself. This comes out in another prophetic picture of the coming Christ, in Isaiah 61:10: *"I will greatly rejoice in the LORD, my soul shall be joyful in my God."* This picture is of the coming Messiah. Our Lord Himself said that the opening verses of this chapter referred to Himself. (See Isaiah 61:1–2; Luke 4:17–21.) This was the deepest source of Christ's joy—God Himself. Joy in the Person of God was His supreme joy.

Joy in God is joy unchangeable and inexhaustible. This joy is also open to us. When we find true joy in the Father, nothing can take it away; for, however circumstances may change, God is ever the same, and He is infinite. The joy that is rooted in Him partakes of His own infinitude. Whether we hang upon a cross or sit upon a throne, our joy, if it is in the infinite God, will be *"unspeakable and full of glory"* (1 Peter 1:8). As Polycarp, who was burned at the stake at age ninety-five for his faith, writhed in physical agony, he cried, "Welcome, cross of Christ; welcome, eternal life." Like his Master's, his joy was in God.

His Unconquerable Optimism

Let us now look at one more feature of Christ that God portrays in His Word—His unconquerable optimism. We shall see that our Lord Jesus was not only the world's greatest saint, savior, and teacher, but He was also the world's greatest optimist. His optimism was not of the shallow kind that is so common, ostentatious, and blatant today, the kind of optimism that comes from closing one's eyes to clearly evident facts. His optimism was the optimism that comes by seeing the facts of this life in the wise and loving and farseeing purpose of God. His clear eyes of faith were focused on an infinitely wise, loving, and powerful God.

A striking portrayal of the unconquerable optimism of the real Christ, the coming Messiah, is recorded in Isaiah 42:4: *"He shall not fail nor be discouraged, till he have set judgment in the earth: and the isles shall wait for his law."* There were many things that could have discouraged Him. He knew that He would be opposed by all the ecclesiastical, political, and military forces of the day. He knew that He would be betrayed by one of His own chosen disciples and denied by another, every one of them forsaking Him. He knew that He would be subjected to such losses and agonies and suffering and shame as no other man has ever endured on this earth; but, in the face of it all, He refused to be in the least bit discouraged, knowing that God reigned and would *"set judgment in the earth."* He knew that *"the isles"* would *"wait for his law,"* though it would take His own ignominious death to accomplish it. He saw the God-ward side—the bright side—of everything.

How the Optimism of Christ Manifested Itself

In His Ability to Look On the Bright Side

In the first place, the unconquerable optimism of the real Christ was manifested in His ability to see the bright side of fierce persecution. In His Sermon on the Mount, Jesus said,

> *Blessed are they which are persecuted for righteousness' sake: for theirs is the kingdom of heaven. Blessed are ye, when men shall revile you, and persecute you, and shall say all manner of evil against you falsely, for my sake. Rejoice, and be exceeding glad: for great is your reward in heaven: for so persecuted they the prophets which were before you.* (Matthew 5:10–12)

To the average mind, harsh persecution does not seem like a bright thing. But it did not weigh down on the mind of Christ, because He saw the God-ward side of it and, therefore, the glorious outcome of it.

So should we. We should not whine over our persecutions but shout over them, even as the Lord Jesus commanded us:

Blessed are ye, when men shall hate you, and when they shall separate you from their company, and shall reproach you, and cast out your name as evil, for the Son of man's sake. Rejoice ye in that day, and leap for joy: for, behold, your reward is great in heaven: for in the like manner did their fathers unto the prophets.   (Luke 6:22–23)

We must remind ourselves that *"the sufferings of this present time are not worthy to be compared with the glory which shall be revealed in us"* (Romans 8:18), and that *"our light affliction, which is but for a moment, worketh for us a far more exceeding and eternal weight of glory"* (2 Corinthians 4:17). Furthermore, we find in the Word, *"If we suffer, we shall also reign with him"* (2 Timothy 2:12), and that if *"we suffer with him, [we will] be also glorified together"* (Romans 8:17).

In His Ability to See
the Achievements of His Death

Second, the unconquerable optimism of Christ Jesus manifested itself in His ability to see that His ignominious death procured blessings for others. We see this in John 12:31–33: *"Now is the judgment of this world: now shall the prince of this world be cast out. And I, if I be lifted up from the earth, will draw all men unto me. This he said, signifying what death he should die."* Our Lord was facing the cross when He uttered these words. The cross was drawing nigh. He saw the agony that He would soon bear on the cross, but He fastened His whole attention on the cross's outcome. He saw the cross as a mighty magnet that would draw all races, kinds, and conditions of men unto Himself, and He saw the cross as the judgment of the Prince of Darkness—the end of Satan's power. He saw that through His own death, He would *"destroy him that had the power of death, that is, the devil"* (Hebrews 2:14).

We also should see, in whatever appalling sufferings we may be called upon to endure for Christ, the good to other men and the glory to God that are to come through our suffering. Then we can be optimistic, even in a fiery furnace. In John 12:24, we read, "*Verily, verily, I say unto you, Except a corn of wheat fall into the ground and die, it abideth alone: but if it die, it bringeth forth much fruit.*" Again, we see Jesus Christ bidding us to follow Him, for He continues, "*He that loveth his life shall lose it; and he that hateth his life in this world shall keep it unto life eternal. If any man serve me, let him follow me; and where I am, there shall also my servant be: if any man serve me, him will my Father honour*" (John 12:25–26).

In His Ability to Focus on
the Prize Awaiting Him After Death

Third, the unconquerable optimism of Jesus, the Christ of God, manifested itself in His ability to focus on the prize He would receive after His death. This we see in John 14:28, where He said to His disciples, in view of His fast-approaching death, "*Ye have heard how I said unto you, I go away, and come again unto you. If ye loved me, ye would rejoice, because I said, I go unto the Father.*" In His death, as terrible as it was to be, He saw the door through which He would pass to be with His eternal Father, the object of His eternal and infinite love. In the same way, and at a later time, the apostle Paul regarded his own death, as terrible as it would be, as the greater good for him, for "*to depart, and to be with Christ…[would be] far better*" (Philippians 1:23).

In His Anticipation of His Glorious Resurrection

Fourth, the unconquerable optimism of our Lord manifested itself in His anticipation of the glorious resurrection that would follow His ignominious death. We see this eager expectation various times in the gospel. For example, we read in John 2:19, *"Jesus answered and said unto them, Destroy this temple, and in three days I will raise it up."* We see it again in John 16:20–22, where our Lord said to His disciples on the night before His crucifixion,

> *Verily, verily, I say unto you, That ye shall weep and lament, but the world shall rejoice: and ye shall be sorrowful, but your sorrow shall be turned into joy. A woman when she is in travail hath sorrow, because her hour is come: but as soon as she is delivered of the child, she remembereth no more the anguish, for joy that a man is born into the world. And ye now therefore have sorrow: but I will see you again, and your heart shall rejoice, and your joy no man taketh from you.*

In His Eagerness to Sit at the Father's Right Hand

Fifth, the unconquerable optimism of the real Christ manifested itself in His eagerness to sit at the right hand of the Father. When He was on trial for His life before Caiaphas, with death at His door, He looked forward to the time when He would sit at the right hand of power, coming on the clouds of heaven. This we see in Matthew 26:62–64:

> *And the high priest arose, and said unto him, Answerest thou nothing? what is it which these witness against thee? But Jesus held his peace. And the high priest answered and said unto him, I adjure thee by the living God, that thou tell us whether thou be the Christ, the Son of God. Jesus saith unto him, Thou hast said: nevertheless I say unto you, Hereafter shall ye see the Son of man sitting on the right hand of power, and coming in the clouds of heaven.*

Recall the scene when they had arrested Jesus and had smitten Him. (See John 18:22.) He knew that they were soon to spit in His face, tear out His beard, scourge Him, and nail Him to the cross. But He looked beyond it all to the day when He would be seated at the right hand of God and return to earth in God's own chariot, on *"the clouds of heaven,"* with all heaven's glorious armies following in His train. We, too, should look beyond the present loss and suffering and shame that are involved in true discipleship, to the day when we will sit down with Christ on His throne. (See Revelation 3:21.)

In His Presence

Sixth, the unconquerable optimism of the true Christ, Christ Jesus, manifested itself in His ability see the wickedness of the world as a precursor of the glad and glorious day of the King's return to save this wrecked and ruined society of ours and to transform it into the fit and eternal abode of God. For example, He looks upon the turmoil and discord and chaos of our world as the logical and inevitable outcome of having rejected and crucified its rightful King. And He looks forward to the glorious resurrection that is to follow. This comes out in a very striking way in Luke 21:25–28:

> *And there shall be signs in the sun, and in the moon, and in the stars; and upon the earth distress of nations, with perplexity; the sea and the waves roaring; men's hearts failing them for fear, and for looking after those things which are coming on the earth: for the powers of heaven shall be shaken. And then shall they see the Son of man coming in a cloud with power and great glory. And when these things begin to come to pass, then look up, and lift up your heads; for your redemption draweth nigh.*

As this earth's history darkens, we, too, should have hearts that are becoming more and more buoyant with hope—hope that is built upon God's prophetic vision. We are told what to do *"when these things begin to come to pass."* What things? The things just described: distress of nations, in perplexity for the roaring of the sea and the billows; men fainting for fear, and for expectation of the things which are coming on the world, the things that cause the hearts of thoughtful statesmen to faint for fear and for expectation of the things that are coming upon human society. What shall we do? Hang our heads? No. Tremble? No. Be afraid? No. *"Lift up your heads; for your redemption draweth nigh."*

Men and women, listen! The world's golden age lies in the future, not in the past—the near future, at that; not the remote future. These things that are happening today in Russia, Poland, Germany, Italy, France, England, America, and elsewhere all shout aloud, *"Your redemption draweth nigh."* We have waited long, but redemption is coming fast. These are great days in which we are living. Great, not because of men's braggart boasting of "big" drives for money, "the *biggest* thing the church of Christ has ever undertaken"—which is a lie, an outrageous and infamous lie—but great because the trumpets of God's fast-accumulating providences proclaim, "The King cometh, God's King."

10

HIS PRAYERFULNESS

*"Who in the days of his flesh, when he had offered up prayers
and supplications with strong crying and tears unto him that was
able to save him from death, and was heard in that he feared."*
—Hebrews 5:7

*"And it came to pass in those days, that he went out into a
mountain to pray, and continued all night in prayer to God."*
—Luke 6:12

Thus far, we have studied eleven very marked characteristics of
the real Christ—the Christ of God's own appointment, the Christ
of actual fact as distinguished from the Christ of popular fancy and
philosophical and mystical speculation, the Christ whose coming
and conduct God gave His chosen prophets of the Old Testament.
God inspired historians to record His life with marvelous accuracy
and fullness in the astonishingly brief but complete records in the
four Gospels. We have studied His holiness, His love for God the
Father, His love for men, His love for souls, His compassion, His

meekness, His humility, His manliness, His imperturbable peace, His constant joyfulness, and His unconquerable optimism. We have not dwelt, as we well might, upon His geniality, His sociability, His friendliness, and His love for home life.

Just let me say that Christ Jesus, the real Christ, was no ascetic and self-absorbed mystic. He loved society and His fellow men. He was a welcome guest at many social and festive gatherings. His first miracle, in which He *"manifested forth his glory"* (John 2:11), was performed at a wedding feast and for the distinct purpose of saving that joyous and festive occasion from ending in embarrassment, disappointment, and gloom. (See John 2:1–11.) He often returned to Bethany for the solace of congenial human companionship and the restful gladness of the genial joys of home life. (See John 11:5.) Even on His last visit to Jerusalem, with the cross only six days ahead of Him, He attended a feast that His friends in Bethany prepared for Him. (See John 12:1–2.)

Furthermore, when Christ went to the garden of Gethsemane for its awful conflict and agonies, He longed for human companionship. He not only took the Eleven to the garden, but He also took a chosen three into the deeper depths of His sorrow. He was a winsome Friend as well as a mighty Savior and the absolute Lord of majestic mien. Did He not say during His last hours, *"Henceforth I call you not servants...but... friends"* (John 15:15)?

As we look now at the wondrous picture of the Christ that God has given to us in the Bible, I invite you to carefully and earnestly consider a characteristic that stands out more prominently than almost any other and underlies all those already mentioned: His prayerfulness. I approach this subject with more hesitation than any other we have looked at because it takes us into the Holy of Holies of His life, where we must take off our shoes and tread softly.

The words *pray* and *prayer* were used at least twenty-five times in connection with Christ in the four Gospels, not to mention other examples in the rest of Scripture. The life of Christ, as we have seen, had many marked characteristics, but nothing is more marked than His prayerfulness. In the book *In His Steps*,[4] written some years ago, Charles Sheldon tried to picture what Jesus would do in various situations if He were still on earth today. It was largely pure and entirely unwarranted imagination; but as the Lord Jesus is *"the same yesterday, and to day, and for ever"* (Hebrews 13:8), I know one thing that He would do if He were physically on this earth today, one occupation in which He would expend very much time and a great deal of physical and mental energy—prayer. I do not know how He would conduct a newspaper. I do not think He would conduct one at all. But I do know that He would pray, pray, pray. And the one who does not spend much time in prayer is not walking "in His steps."

How the Prayerfulness of the Real Christ Was Manifested

Let us consider first how the prayerfulness of the real Christ—not the Christ of man's imagination, but the Christ of indubitable historic fact—was manifested.

In His Diligence in Prayer

First, the prayerfulness of the real Christ, the Christ of the Bible, the Christ of God's own Word, was manifested in His diligence in prayer to God. We read in Luke's gospel *"that he went out into a mountain to pray, and continued all night in prayer to God"* (Luke 6:12). On another occasion, our Lord spent time in prayer

4. See Charles Sheldon, *In His Steps* (New Kensington, PA: Whitaker House, 1980).

from about sunset until after three o'clock in the morning. (See Mark 6:45–48.) This whole night of prayer followed a day of intense and wearying activity.

On this busy day, Christ had not eaten, and He had taken His disciples aside to *"rest a while"* (Mark 6:31). However, it was not long before the crowd found Him and sought out His teaching. Instead of resting, He spent the day preaching to the multitude, healing the sick, and feeding the hungry. That night, He did not slip into a deep slumber but stayed awake to pray to the Father. There is often a better way to recuperate exhausted energies than by sleep. It would be far more beneficial to rise and pour our hearts out to God when we cannot fall sleep, instead of wasting time tossing to and fro upon our beds. We would get far more rest and go back to bed quieted, for *"he giveth his beloved sleep"* (Psalm 127:2). Although not every night of our Lord's life was spent in prayer, many of them were. Here, too, we might wisely follow Him.

In His Morning Ritual

Second, the prayerfulness of Christ Jesus was manifested in His habit of waking up early to pray in a solitary place before the beginning of the day. We read of one occasion that *"in the morning, rising up a great while before day, he went out, and departed into a solitary place, and there prayed"* (Mark 1:35). This particular instance took place the morning after a very busy day. The day before, He had taught in the synagogue in Capernaum, healed a man possessed with an unclean spirit, and then had gone to the house of Simon and Andrew to heal Simon's mother-in-law. As the sun began to set, the people, hearing of the wondrous things He had done, came flocking to Simon's house to bring Him *"all that were diseased, and them that were possessed with devils"* (Mark 1:32). In fact, we read that *"all the city was gathered together at the door"* (Mark 1:33), and that He *"healed many that were sick of divers diseases, and cast out many devils"* (Mark 1:35). But, as exhausting as the day had been, and as late as He had retired that night, He rose up long before the next day and went to the desert so that He could pray undisturbed. Happy is the man who has learned this secret from the Lord—the secret of getting alone with God early in the morning, while others are still sleeping, so that he might have undisturbed communion with God and plenty time for prayer.

If we would do this, we would be more like Christ in our characters and conduct, as well as be more effective in our service. I read years ago that one of the most successful statesmen England has ever produced, Earl of Cairns, Lord Chancellor of England, said that he attributed all his success to the time he spent in the Word of God and in prayer. He would spend two hours every morning with the Lord. When I was in England, I had the privilege of meeting the widow of Lord Cairns for dinner and taking her out to the repast. After the dinner was over, I said to her, "Lady Cairns, I read some years ago that your husband said that he spent two hours every day studying the Bible and praying and attributed all of his success in life to these practices. Is that true?" Lady Cairns replied, "I cannot say positively about the two hours, but this I do know, that whatever hour of night we reached home from parliament (I always went with him, and we always rode home together), whatever hour it was, midnight, one, two, or three o'clock in the morning, he always arose at the same early hour in the morning [I think she said it was six o'clock] and shut himself up alone with his God and with his Bible." And she added, "When he was a member of Lord Disraeli's cabinet and there was a stormy session, Disraeli would say upon my husband's entrance, 'Now we will have peace, the Earl of Cairns has come.'"

In His Preparation Through Prayer

Third, the prayerfulness of Christ Jesus was manifested in the way He used prayer to prepare for the crises and great events in

His life. In Luke 3:21, we are told that the heavens were opened as He was praying. This is when *"the Holy Ghost descended in a bodily shape like a dove upon him and, a voice came from heaven, which said, Thou art my beloved Son; in thee I am well pleased."*

So we see that He prayed before He was baptized and began ministering to the public. In Mark 1:35–38, we see Him praying before the beginning of an evangelistic tour. In Luke 6:12–13, we see Him spending a night in prayer before choosing the twelve disciples whom He would train to be the leaders in the early church. Luke also tells us in chapter 9 of his gospel that it was after a special season of prayer with His disciples that Christ announced His approaching death.

Evidently, He prepared for all the great events and crises of life through seasons of intensive prayer. There is a lesson here for us to learn, a much-needed lesson. Thirty denominations in this country have recently launched what they claim to be "the biggest thing the church of Christ has ever undertaken." They are putting many dollars into the preliminary campaign to raise the money and are doing more advertising than many of the greatest business corporations ever have. And what are their prayer preparations for this mighty event? The Christians of the land were urged in thousands of newspaper advertisements to spend *five minutes* in secret prayer on the day the campaign was launched. This should be ludicrous and perhaps even heartbreaking to those who really know the real Christ and the way He lived His life.

In His Times of Solitude

Fourth, the prayerfulness of the Christ was manifested in the times of solitude He spent with the Father after moments of great achievement. This we see illustrated in Matthew 14:23: *"And when he had sent the multitudes away, he went up into a mountain apart to pray: and when the evening was come, he was there alone."* This time of prayer followed a day filled with marvelous displays of divine compassion and power. He had healed multitudes of sick people and displayed His divine creative power by feeding *"five thousand men, beside women and children"* (Matthew 14:21) with five small loaves and two small fish! The multitudes were amazed by His wondrous power. They wished to make Him King on the spot. But no, He wanted none of their applause. He dismissed them, along with the disciples, and went to a secluded part of the mountain to pray, spending nine hours alone with God.

Why? First of all, so that He might renew His strength. Christ spent His power on others when He performed miracles. (See Mark 5:30.) Furthermore, He spent time with the Father to fight the temptation to entertain pride or self-satisfaction or contentment with what He had done.

Let us never forget that our Lord Jesus, while He was very God of very God, was also a real man, subject to the same temptations that we are. Therefore, in order to set an example for us, He met His temptations with the same weapons we must use—the Word of God and prayer. What a lesson for us! It is more likely that most of us come to God before great events rather than after them, but the latter is just as important as the former. If only we would really pray after the great achievements of life, we might go on to even greater achievements. But if we do not, we are either puffed up or exhausted by them; and so we proceed to no greater achievements.

In His Habit of Withdrawing

Fifth, the prayerfulness of Christ Jesus was manifested in His habit of withdrawing from the crowd and going to a solitary place to pray. This we see, for example, in Luke 5:15–16: *"But so much the more went there a fame abroad of him: and great multitudes came together to hear, and to be healed by him of their infirmities. And he withdrew himself into the wilderness, and prayed."* How unlike Him we are. We would have thought this to be the time of opportunity, the time to cultivate the crowd, the day to stay with them, the time to work and not to pray (as if praying were not the mightiest kind of work). But this was not so with our Lord. This was the time He needed God and went away to talk to Him.

Some men are "so busy" that they "can find no time to pray." It seemed, though, that the busier Christ's life was—the more crowded with necessary activity—the more He prayed. There were times when He had no time to eat (see Mark 3:20; 6:31) and occasions when He had no time to rest or sleep (see Mark 6:33, 46), but He still had time to pray. The more work He had to do, the more He prayed. Many mighty men have learned this secret from Christ, but many other men have lost their power because they have not learned this secret. Like the Master, may we not allow our busy schedules to crowd out prayer in our lives.

In His Use of Prayer in Resisting Temptation

Sixth, the prayerfulness of Christ Jesus was manifested in the way He used prayer to prepare Himself for temptation. We see a remarkable illustration of this in Luke 22:39–41:

> *And he came out, and went, as he was wont, to the mount of Olives; and his disciples also followed him. And when he was at the place, he said unto them, Pray that ye enter not into temptation. And he was withdrawn from them about a stone's cast, and kneeled down, and prayed.*

He prepared for temptations by praying so that He was always victorious. The disciples, despite His solemn warning, slept while He prayed. Therefore, when the storm came, they fell instead of stood. The calm majesty of His bearing amid the awful onslaughts of Pilate's judgment at Calvary was the outcome of His prayer.

In His Practice of Taking Everything to God

Seventh, the prayerfulness of Jesus Christ was manifested in His practice of lifting up the most ordinary matters of everyday life to God. Over and over again, our attention is called to the fact that He prayed about anything and everything, even the most ordinary meal. (See, for example, Matthew 14:19). Indeed, so characteristic was His manner of praying in connection with His everyday meals that the two disciples He encountered on the road to Emmaus after the resurrection failed to recognize Him until He lifted His eyes to pray to God before breaking the bread, at which point they knew Him instantly. (See Luke 24:13–16, 30–31.) For most of us, it is in connection with the little things that we most frequently forget to pray. Every step of Christ's life seems to have been accompanied with prayer and sanctified in prayer.

In His Final Earthly Utterance

Eighth, the prayerfulness of Jesus Christ was manifested in His last earthly utterance. As Christ breathed His last breath and gave up His spirit to God, He cried, *"Father, into thy hands I commend my spirit"* (Luke 23:46). And that was not the only prayer He breathed while He was on the cross. (See verse 34.) His life had been a continuous prayer.

Our Lord Jesus undoubtedly loved human society; nevertheless, in His deep sense of need to commune with God, we often see Him fleeing from the crowds to go pray in a solitary place, such as the hidden recesses of the mountains. (See Matthew 14:23.) Each of the four evangelists mentioned His going to the mountains to pray. In relation to this habit, Luke writes, *"As his custom was"* (Luke 22:39 rv). In *Imago Christi*, James Stalker wrote, "When He arrived in a town, His first thought was, which was the shortest road to the mountain,—just as ordinary travellers inquire where are the most noted sights and which is the best hotel."[5] He prayed alone by Himself (see Matthew 14:23), with a chosen few (see Luke 9:28), with the whole apostolic company (see Luke 9:18), and in the midst of a great multitude (see Matthew 14:19).

How Jesus Christ Prayed

We shall get no adequate conception of the prayer life of the Christ of God without considering the question of how He prayed. The Bible has much to say about this.

With God's Glory in View

First, Christ Jesus prayed with God's glory in view. He prayed so that God might be glorified, should He answer the prayer. This we see in that marvelous prayer He offered in the presence of His disciples just before He was arrested. He began His prayer with these words: *"Father, the hour is come; glorify thy Son, that thy Son also may glorify thee"* (John 17:1). We see the same thing in the prayer He taught His disciples, which begins with the words, *"Our Father which art in heaven, hallowed be thy name"* (Matthew 6:9; Luke 11:2).

In Accordance with the Father's Will

Second, Jesus Christ prayed in accordance with the Father's will. This we see in His cry of agony in the garden: *"O my Father, if this cup may not pass away from me, except I drink it, thy will be done"* (Matthew 26:42).

---

5. James Stalker, *Imago Christi: The Example of Jesus Christ* (New York: A. C. Armstrong & Son, 1892), 131.

With the Proper Posture

Third, as to the posture which He assumed in prayer, He sometimes prayed standing (see John 11:41–42; 17:1; 14:31; 18:1); sometimes kneeling (see Luke 22:41); sometimes lying on His face before God (see Matthew 26:39). If the sinless Son of God got down upon His knees, yes, upon His face before God, what attitude should we ordinary mortals assume as we go into God's presence?

With Intense Earnestness

Fourth, He prayed with intense earnestness. This we see in Luke 22:44: *"And being in an agony he prayed more earnestly: and his sweat was as it were great drops of blood falling down to the ground."* The literal meaning of the word translated *"earnestly"* actually means "stretched-out-edly." This verse says that Christ's soul was "stretched out" in intense agony before the Lord.

We see the same thing in Hebrews 5:7: *"Who in the days of his flesh, when he had offered up prayers and supplications with strong crying and tears unto him that was able to save him from death, and was heard in that he feared."* We see Christ's intense earnestness in the words *"prayers and supplications."* The word translated *"prayers"* is a strong and expressive word that refers to the expression of a felt need, somewhat like an entreaty. The word translated *"supplications"* is not found anywhere else in the New Testament. It is a peculiarly significant word, meaning "imploring supplications." But the intense earnestness of the Lord's Prayer comes out still more clearly in the words *"with strong crying and tears."* The word translated *"crying"* is a very strong word, meaning "outcry" or "clamor," the force of which is increased by the qualifying adjective *"strong."* Literally translated, it would read that He prayed with a "mighty outcry."

There are some who speak of it as an attainment of superior faith to always be very calm in prayer, "just taking" what they ask for in childlike confidence. Those who say this have either surpassed their Master or do not know what Holy Ghost earnestness means. More often than not, their calmness comes from indifference instead of the Holy Ghost. The Holy Ghost makes intercessions *"with groanings which cannot be uttered"* (Romans 8:26). In view of the example of our Lord, we need to be careful not to confuse the laziness of indifference with the "rest of faith." Any "rest of faith" that does not leave room for mighty conflicts in prayer and action is not Christlike.

At Great Length

Fifth, our Lord Jesus spent a lot of time in prayer. He often spent whole nights praying. (See Luke 6:12.) How long we pray is of great importance. By the use of modern machinery, a man can do in a minute what he once could do in hours; but no machinery has ever been invented nor ever will be invented that can expedite the work of prayer. Effective prayer demands time—much time—and woe to those who let business take away from their prayer time.

With Importunity

Sixth, Jesus Christ prayed importunately—that is, He repeatedly asked for the same thing. We see this in Matthew 26:44: *"He left them, and went away again, and prayed the third time, saying the same words."* We see in the example of our Lord in this matter that it will not do to say, as so many do, that the failure to take what you ask for, the first time you ask for it, necessarily indicates weak faith. It indicated no weakness of faith on the part of our Lord that in His intense earnestness and in the determination of faith, He uttered precisely the same petition three times in the garden of Gethsemane.

With Thanksgiving

Seventh, our Lord prayed with thanksgiving. We see this when he prayed before the raising of Lazarus from the dead.

> *Then they took away the stone from the place where the dead was laid. And Jesus lifted up his eyes, and said, Father, I thank thee that thou hast heard me. And I knew that thou hearest me always: but because of the people which stand by I said it, that they may believe that thou hast sent me.*
>
> (John 11:41–42)

In this case, we see that Christ thanked God in advance for the answer to prayer before He actually received it.

With Belief

Eighth, our Lord prayed believingly. He prayed with the absolute certainty that He had received from God the petition that He asked of Him. We see this in the previous passage, where Jesus said, "*I thank thee that thou hast heard me*"—before Lazarus had risen from the grave! He believed; He had no doubt; He "knew" that the Father would grant His every request.

We see John, the beloved disciple, following in the footsteps of his Master's faith in 1 John 3:22, where he wrote, "*And whatsoever we ask, we receive of him, because we keep his commandments, and do those things that are pleasing in his sight.*" We, too, should learn to rest upon God's promise, ask in accordance with His will, and believe that we have received what we have asked for.

What a striking contrast there is between the prayer of the real Christ—Christ Jesus—and the prayer of "Christ," the "Christ principle" of Christian Science. Mrs. Mary Baker Grover Patterson Eddy scoffed at the thought that there was a personal God who answered prayer. What Christian Scientists sometimes call "prayer" is not, in proper sense, prayer at all. It is merely concentrated, self-willed thinking. It denies the existence of the things from which Christian Scientists wish deliverance, whether sickness, pain, sin, death, or misfortune of any kind. Their substitute for prayer—"demonstrating the truth," as they sometimes call it—has landed many in the grave, many others in divorce courts, many others in the lunatic asylum. I hold in my hand a copy of *Science and Health* that was given to Mr. Jacoby when we were holding a united evangelistic campaign in 1908. It was given to him by a man who said Christian Science had robbed him of his wife and daughter and had wrecked his home. In giving the book to Mr. Jacoby, he said, "This has nearly landed me in the insane asylum." But the true Christ, the Christ of God, the Lord Jesus, really prayed. His prayers wrought miracles, healed the sick, cast out demons, raised the dead, glorified God, and helped Him to finish the work God gave Him to do.

We have come to the end of our studies of the wonderful picture of the real Christ that God has given us in His Word. Let us follow Him. Let us follow Him in His holiness; let us follow Him in His love for the Father; let us follow Him in His love for men; let us follow Him in His love for souls; let us follow Him in His compassion; let us follow Him in His meekness; let us follow Him in His humility; let us follow Him in His manliness; let us follow Him in His imperturbable peace; let us follow Him in His constant joyfulness; let us follow Him in His unconquerable optimism; and, above all, let us follow Him in His prayerfulness, which, in many ways was the secret of all the other beauties and glories of His peerless life. It was the secret to His divine life that was lived as a real man here on this earth.

Christ lived under the same conditions that you and I live under, with the same temptations that we face, and with the complete victory that can be yours and mine, also. And, while we pray intensely, often in long vigils in a solitary place alone with God, let us never forget that closing prayer that God's Word teaches us—our prayer of response to the closing promise of God's Word, "*Surely I come quickly*": "*Amen. Even so, come, Lord Jesus*" (Revelation 22:20). For, when He comes, we shall be perfected in holiness, in love for the Father, in love for our fellow man, in love for souls, in compassion, in meekness, in humility, in manliness, in peace, in joy, in optimism, and in every grace and perfection and glory of Christ's character. When He comes, "*we shall be like him; for we shall see him as he is*" (1 John 3:2).

ABOUT THE AUTHOR

Reuben Archer Torrey (1856–1928) was born in Hoboken, New Jersey, on January 28, 1856. He graduated from Yale University in 1875 and from Yale Divinity School in 1878.

Upon his graduation, Dr. Torrey became a Congregational minister. A few years later, he joined Dwight L. Moody in his evangelistic work in Chicago and became the pastor of the Chicago Avenue Church. He was selected by D. L. Moody to become the first dean of the Moody Bible Institute of Chicago. Under his direction, Moody Institute became a pattern for Bible institutes around the world.

Torrey is respected as one of the greatest evangelists of modern times. At the turn of the century, he began his evangelistic tours and crusades. He spent the years of 1903–1905 in a worldwide revival campaign, along with the famous song leader Charles McCallon Alexander. Together, they ministered in many parts of the world, and reportedly brought nearly one-hundred-thousand souls to Jesus. Torrey continued worldwide crusades for the next fifteen years, eventually reaching Japan and China. During those same years, he served as Dean of the Bible Institute of Los Angeles and pastored the Church of the Open Door in that city.

Torrey longed for more Christian workers to take an active part in bringing the message of salvation through Christ to a lost and dying world. His straightforward style of evangelism has shown thousands of Christian workers how to become effective soulwinners.

Dr. Torrey died on October 26, 1928. He is well remembered today for his inspiring devotional books on the Christian life, which have been translated into many different languages. Woven throughout his many books, the evangelistic message that sent Torrey around the world still ministers to all whose hearts yearn to lead men, women, and children to salvation through Jesus Christ.